D0090236

Why Do I Eat When I'm Not Hungry?

Why Do I Eat When I'm Not Hungry?

How to Use Your Body's Own Energy System to Treat Food Addictions with the Revolutionary Callahan Techniques

Roger Callahan, Ph.D.
with Paul Perry

DOUBLEDAY
New York   London   Toronto   Sydney   Auckland

PUBLISHED BY DOUBLEDAY
a division of Bantam Doubleday Dell Publishing Group, Inc.
666 Fifth Avenue, New York, New York 10103

The exercises in Chapter 12 are from
Total Fitness in Thirty Minutes a Week,
copyright © 1975 by Laurence E. Morehouse, Ph.D.
Reprinted by permission of Simon & Schuster, Inc.

For further information about
Dr. Callahan's work, call The National
Center for the Rapid Treatment of Anxiety at
800-359-C-U-R-E,
or write to:
45350 Vista Santa Rosa,
Indian Wells, CA 92210.

The Callahan Techniques is a registered
trademark of Dr. Roger Callahan.

Library of Congress Cataloging-in-Publication Data

Callahan, Roger
    Why do I eat when I'm not hungry? : how to use your own energy
system to treat food addictions with the revolutionary
Callahan techniques / Roger Callahan with Paul Perry.
        p.   cm.
        1. Compulsive eating.   2. Rehabilitation.   I. Perry, Paul   II. Title.
RC552.C65C35   1991
    616.85′26—dc20   91-2230
                                                                          CIP

ISBN 0-385-41824-8

Book Design by Richard Oriolo

Illustrations by Jackie Aher

FIRST EDITION

To Jennifer, Ryan, and Caitlin

ACKNOWLEDGMENTS

I want to thank the unknown genius of the Orient who first found that the body possesses energy systems that can be used to help people get over their ills. This important discovery was made about five or six thousand years ago, and we of the West are just beginning to appreciate its potential power.

Without the brilliant discoveries of Dr. George Goodheart in the field of applied kinesiology, my work would not have been possible. He is not, of course, responsible for any errors I have made in my field of clinical psychology. The rigorous scholarly and original work of Dr. David Walther in the field of applied kinesiology has also been a source of inspiration and help to me.

I am indebted to the basic scientific work of Dr. Bjorn Nordenstrom of Sweden and Dr. Robert O. Becker of New York, relating to the energy system. Although my work is not directly related, their research helps provide a solid theoretical foundation for all work in the field of body energy.

I want to thank Paul Perry for shaping my ideas into a more readable form and for his cheerful disposition, which made our work together pleasurable. Thanks to Nat Sobel, a stellar agent, for putting it all together.

It was a source of great comfort and a great privilege to have the editorial help and wisdom of Judy Kern.

Many thanks are due to Joanne Laughrin, my associate, for her generous help and loving support.

RJC

CONTENTS

Part I

Part II

Why Do I Eat When I'm Not Hungry?

Part I

ONE

Discovering the Callahan Techniques

Do you eat when you shouldn't? Most of us do. Ten years ago I found out why we do that. More important, I found a powerful, natural, quick treatment to eliminate your urge to eat even though you may be climbing the walls or lusting intensely to eat something when you shouldn't. The treatment takes less than a minute.

Before this discovery, I was just another frustrated psychologist. I had a practice in Los Angeles, California, working with patients who had a variety of problems. There were phobics, people with an unreasonable fear of things like water and heights, people who wanted to reach their full potential but felt blocked by something that had happened in their lives, and there were food addicts—people who came in and asked, "Why do I eat when I'm not hungry?"

At the time I couldn't tell them exactly why they ate too much. But of course I tried. I guessed that their mothers had convinced them to eat for comfort and they had never stopped. I told them that there was too much readily available food around and maybe they should learn to live with an emptier refrigerator. I told them to read instead of eat. To walk instead of eat. To go to bed instead of eat. To have sex instead of eat. I even had them try hypnosis and acupuncture.

For the most part this is what all psychologists do. They give this advice to people singly or in groups, but the advice is almost always the same when it comes to food addiction—do something besides eat.

The results are almost always the same, too. After losing a few pounds or maybe quite a few pounds the patient gains back all that he or she has lost and then some. This is a syndrome known as "yo-yo" dieting. It is really one of the shames of the weight loss business.

I had a lot of yo-yo dieters among my patients. All psychologists who deal with food addicts do. Probably 90 percent of the people I treated who lost weight would gain it back within a year. Numbers like that are common in weight loss treatment. In fact a study published by a team of researchers from the University of Pennsylvania showed that 98 percent of the people who lose weight on liquid fasts regain their weight to within five pounds. This study led the president of a diet formula company to say, "Last year, everybody knew somebody who lost one hundred pounds on a liquid fast. Now everybody knows somebody who lost one hundred pounds and gained back one hundred and twenty."

This isn't a criticism of the people who work in weight loss treatment. Getting people to lose weight and keep it off is very difficult in a society that prides itself on an abundant supply of food.

Still I was frustrated. Like all psychologists, I like to see improvement in my patients. In the case of food addicts that means long-term weight loss, not just a dip in weight that lasts a few months.

In a way, being a psychologist is not unlike being a gardener. We like to see our patients flower and blossom. But a garden in which only 10 percent of the plantings become flowers would not be a very satisfying garden. That is how I felt about dealing with food addicts.

Still, I continued to work with them in the traditional ways of therapy. A 10 percent cure rate is better than nothing at all, I told myself. I continued to look for better, more effective ways of changing their behavior. I tried hypnosis, suggestion, rational emotive therapy, systematic desensitization, aversion therapy—anything that might work. No matter what I tried, patients gained back the weight they lost and then some within about six months of extensive therapy. Maybe that should read "expensive" therapy. It cost my patients a lot of money to lose just a few pounds.

Then I discovered something that changed the nature of my garden, if you will. Through the work of Dr. George Goodheart, the first chiropractor to be a member of the U.S. Olympic Medical Team, I came across the body of knowledge known as *applied kinesiology*, a field he discovered. Applied kinesiology deals with the way in which the body's electrical energy—regular flows of electricity called *meridians* by practitioners of acupuncture—affects the well-being of the physical body. Many physical problems, Goodheart reasons, are a result of the body's electrical systems' having gone awry. By working on these meridians with techniques similar to acupressure, practitioners of applied kinesiology can correct bodily dysfunctions.

New Treatment Revealed

Dr. Harvey Ross, a psychiatrist and friend, was the first to show me one of the diagnostic techniques used by applied kinesiologists to demonstrate the effects of positive and negative thoughts on this electrical system. I found these techniques to be a monument to simplicity and accuracy. Dr. Ross demonstrated them on me after he had attended a meeting where Goodheart's work was being discussed and demonstrated.

"Hold your arm straight out and resist my pressure," he told me. I did. My arm was resisting the pressure with a springy bounce.

"Now think a negative thought," he said. As I thought about my house being burned down in a fire, he pushed down on my wrist with the same force and my arm dropped, powerless.

I was overwhelmed. Since the phenomenon was inexplicable according to anything known at the time, I was also very curious. I realized that certain muscles appeared to go weak under various conditions, such as thinking negative thoughts. I didn't realize at the time that this had any application to the treatment of food addictions. But I did realize that applied kinesiology—like acupuncture—tapped into an extremely powerful and little-known energy system that could be used to heal physical problems.

Goodheart and other doctors use it to treat physical problems. One of his cases, for instance, was a patient with an extremely weak arm. This man had gone to traditional physicians to find the source of the weakness. Various tests showed nothing physically wrong, but still the weakness persisted. That was when he went to Goodheart.

Goodheart could find nothing wrong, either. But there was a distinct difference in strength between the man's arms. Since he appeared to have no psychological problems, the doctor decided to carry his search further than he normally would have. He began to probe the man's meridians. He knew the location of these meridians from his knowledge of acupuncture, the ancient Chinese medicine that manipulates these electrical fields with needles to cure many problems. When he had the man touch a point on the meridian related to the man's arm, the weakness disappeared. This led him to something known as "therapy localization," which allowed for a greater precision in the diagnosis of many muscular problems.

Applied kinesiologists evaluate how the nervous system controls muscle function. Early practitioners performed muscle tests in which they sought out "strong" or "weak" muscles. The tests were not to evaluate muscle strength, but to show how the nervous system affects the muscles.

The aim of this testing was to correct structural imbalances caused by poorly functioning muscles.

Like practitioners of acupuncture, applied kinesiologists found that the body is divided into a number of meridians, each including some vital organ as well as considerable skin surface. When a meridian becomes blocked, illness or pain may result. Rhythmic tapping at a specific point on the meridian may improve the condition of the associated vital organ. This occurs because the energy flow within that meridian is freed to move again. It is as though blood flow has been reestablished to an organ with blocked arteries.

My First Case

All of this seemed very interesting, especially for those in the medical profession who deal in the physical realm. But as a psychologist, I could see no real use for this knowledge within my practice. Still, I was excited by the discovery of a field that was completely new to me. I took a course in applied kinesiology just to satisfy my curiosity, as well as a number of workshops.

Then one day, out of sheer frustration, I decided to try a variation of applied kinesiology on a patient who had a terrible, lifelong fear of water.

I had treated this woman (whom we'll call Mary) for aquaphobia (fear of water) for more than a year. During that time we had tried everything in my repertoire, and as a result she could take short showers and sit nervously on the side of a swimming pool for a few minutes. But she still had nightmares almost every night that she was being dropped into the middle of an ocean by some mysterious force. She still could not drive on the coast highway with its beautiful view of the Pacific Ocean. Just *seeing* that much water was more than she could bear. Nevertheless, she was happy with this tiny bit of progress.

But I wasn't. I found her tiny bit of progress frustrating. I wanted her to *get into the water. Comfortably. I wanted her problem to be gone.*

I decided to experiment on Mary with some techniques I had developed as a result of thirty years of experience as a therapist and my applied kinesiology research.

I asked her to think about water, and since her phobic reactions usually manifested themselves in her stomach, I asked her to tap a spot that might balance the flow of energy into the stomach.

The treatment took less than two minutes. She said she was cured. In disbelief, I asked her to go to the pool. Instead of dragging her heels, she walked out of my office, which was in my home, and almost ran to the deep end of the swimming pool. "Don't, Mary, look out!" I shouted after her as a reminder that she couldn't swim.

"Dr. Callahan, I know I can't swim," she reassured me. She went to the deep end of the pool, bent down and splashed water on her face. She laughed with delight and happiness.

I was shocked. These meridian taps were certainly not the strangest things I had tried on her. But I really didn't expect them to work so fast, if at all. I was just trying them out.

To prove that she was cured, she later drove down to the beach and waded into the surf. To top it off, she did it on an evening when Los Angeles was experiencing a rare torrential rainstorm, complete with lightning and thunder.

She was cured. Ten years later, she still has no fear of water. The nightmares have vanished.

Further Research

I was so surprised by this remarkable event that I couldn't wait to try the treatment on other clients. I realized that this could be an important new discovery. If it worked on others, I might have found a way to cure phobias quickly. I would later find out that similar treatments, with some variations, could cure addictions, too.

I tried the treatment with other patients. First I worked with phobics, people who experience severe and irrational anxiety over specific things like water, heights, closed spaces, driving over bridges, even things like cats and dogs. There is an almost infinite number of phobias, affecting more than 30 million people, dozens of whom were then my patients.

I tried these unusual techniques on them. Some thought I had cracked up and left for other, more traditional psychotherapists. But the ones who stayed were in for a surprise. *The treatments worked.*

Within minutes, four out of ten phobics were facing their worst nightmares, and they were no longer afraid. People who feared heights went to the tops of buildings. Those who feared water went wading. People who were afraid to drive on freeways did it during rush hour without sweaty palms or palpitating hearts.

Many of these patients were cured with just one or two procedures. Some required more. I developed other treatments for the more difficult cases. With these additional treatments, discovered and developed over the next ten years, I was able to boost my cure rate for simple phobias from about 40 percent to about 98 percent! The treatment usually took just minutes, and the patients appeared to be cured.

A definition of the word "cure" is important here, since the word does not even appear in many psychologic dictionaries. A person is cured when a psychological problem is made to "go away" as a result of the treatment administered by a psychotherapist. Quite simply, if there is no further evidence of the problem, then the patient is cured.

As a psychologist I had been trained to appreciate the incredible complexity of the human psyche, and to live with a far less than perfect rate of cure. So, when my cure rate with phobics approached 100 percent, it was hard for me to believe my own success. I kept reviewing the research data and doubting it myself. Even ten years later, the patients I could locate were still cured as a result of my rapid treatments.

Eventually I came to realize I couldn't deny the facts. Almost everyone I treated for simple delimited phobias was cured.

The Techniques

I called these treatments the "Callahan Techniques." I went on radio and television, where I demonstrated my ability to cure people of common phobias such as fear of public speaking or fear of needles in just a few minutes. I cured people with deep-seated fears of snakes and cats, a woman who was deathly afraid of driving over bridges, and people who were afraid of riding in elevators.

I treated talk show host Tom Snyder for his fear of heights on a major television program. After only two minutes of treatment, he was able to climb fearlessly to the top of a ladder.

"I just don't believe it" is the refrain I hear from many of my patients when they are instantly cured. Even *they* find it hard to believe.

Treating Food Addiction

I was on a radio talk show, working with phobics in the audience, when a man called in and said he was afraid of nothing. "But I am dying to eat right now. Can you help me?" I experimented with a treatment and was able to help him right there on the air. In less than two minutes he had no interest in eating.

Although going from phobics to food addicts may seem like a real leap, I found it isn't. Both these disorders have anxiety at their base.

With a phobic, the source of the anxiety may be irrational, but it is, nevertheless, obvious. In food addicts, anxiety causes the irresistible urge to overeat. Food addicts try to calm themselves (relieve their anxiety) with the comfort of food. Food will mask that anxiety, soothe it, and make it *seem* to go away. But it really doesn't. It is just hidden.

I call this the "anxiety/addiction connection." All addictions are caused by anxiety. The substances or behaviors that you become addicted to—things like thumb-sucking, nail-biting, hair-pulling, drugs, alcohol, or food—are things that "mask" your anxiety. They keep it "covered up" so it doesn't seem to bother you. Hence, food addicts, when they feel a rise in anxiety, eat to mask the anxiety. Food doesn't reduce the anxiety, it only covers it like a blanket. Food addicts are not usually aware that they are anxious; they are aware only of the urge to eat.

Perhaps one of the best examples of the anxiety/addiction connection has to do with the use of heroin by American soldiers during the Vietnam war.

It was reported that a large number of American combat troops were using illegal drugs, including heroin, and that the United States would have to brace itself for a fresh wave of drug addicts when these soldiers returned home. Since heroin is considered physically as well as psychologically addicting, such a warning seemed logical.

When most of the returning soldiers did not continue to use heroin or other hard drugs, the experts were surprised. With the anxiety of combat behind them, our returning soldiers no longer needed to take drugs. The physiological aspect of addiction appeared to be rather insignificant.

About twenty years ago I read a scientific report from

England, where patients suffering severe and chronic pain are legally treated with heroin. When their pain stops, the heroin is stopped too. Surprisingly, the patients show no symptoms of withdrawl.

Professor Ronald Melzack of McGill University is an expert on physical pain. In a dramatic article, "The Tragedy of Needless Pain" *(Scientific American,* February 1990), he attempts to correct the mistaken but widely held belief that patients who take morphine for pain are bound to become addicted.

My belief is that patients who take morphine, or any other drug, for relief of *anxiety* are the ones who get addicted. In other words, addiction is mainly a psychological problem.

I have found food addictions to be mainly psychological as well—an attempt to tranquilize anxiety. Rising anxiety causes the person to search for a tranquilizer. If he finds food soothes him, he becomes addicted to its tranquilizing effects. Sometimes people find their tranquilizer in alcohol, cigarettes, or drugs, especially the legal ones such as Valium or Xanax. Many people have the mistaken idea that tranquilizers cure anxiety. They don't. They merely mask the problem while creating the strong likelihood for addiction.

Surveys have shown that anxiety is the most common psychological problem in the country. Anxiety can have no apparent source, or it can be caused by factors such as job stress or bad traffic. *Chapin's Dictionary of Psychology* defines anxiety as the "feeling of mingled dread and apprehension about the future without specific cause for fear." Many people overeat when their jobs make them nervous, when they are angry at their spouse, when the kids are noisy, when they don't have time to take a walk, or when they are feeling sorry for themselves and Ronald McDonald says, "You deserve a break today." The list of reasons to overeat goes on and on.

One of my patients finds that she overeats only when sitting in the sun. It seems as though "doing nothing," or not being distracted, causes her anxiety level to climb!

Whatever the cause of anxiety, a food addict eats to mask it. And when the addict gets relief, he subconsciously reinforces the addiction. The food doesn't stop the anxiety any more than tranquilizers do; it only masks it. The anxiety is still there, waiting to be "covered up" with food again and again. That is why you eat when you are not hungry.

Weight loss specialists seem to believe that people gain weight because they don't follow the correct diet. They are partly correct, but typically food addicts are *unable* to follow a correct diet. They admit that *losing* weight is easy. But the real trick is keeping the weight off. Experts with the medically based diet program Optifast, which is affiliated with St. Luke's Hospital in New York, have had great success in trimming weight from morbidly obese patients. They do it by putting them on a diet of liquid protein that allows them to lose as much as three to four pounds per week. But when these patients go off the liquid fast diet, they often gain weight as rapidly as they lost it.

Addiction Caused by Anxiety

Some weight loss specialists know that people overeat when they are frustrated or under stress, but they don't seem to realize that food is an addiction and the cause of the addiction is anxiety.

The Callahan Techniques treat anxiety. Without drugs, without pain.

There is another problem I discovered, which is the most formidable villain in treating addiction. It is the problem of psychological reversal, the mental block that causes food addicts to become their own worst enemies.

My First Food Addiction Cure

One of the first food addiction patients I treated with my new techniques was a woman we will call Anne.

She had an addiction to Snickers candy bars. At least three times a day she would pull one of these scrumptious bars from her purse and eat it. Never without her favorite "tranquilizer," she always carried five for "emergencies."

Anne had been told by her doctor that the arm pains she was having were not the result of overwork but of worsening heart disease. He recommended that she cut fat and cholesterol from her diet and try to lose weight.

She quit eating meat and ice cream and other high-fat, high-cholesterol foods. But as hard as she tried, she just couldn't quit eating the Snickers. In other words, she was addicted.

I explained that I wanted to help her stop eating Snickers.

"Im-possible," she said. But she was willing to try anyway. She was craving one right then, she said. On a scale of one to ten, she rated her desire level at a nine. Although this desire level is driven by anxiety, addicts are not aware of the anxiety, they are only aware of their desire for the object of their addiction. In order to monitor the progress of treatment, I always ask the addict to rate his or her desire.

Through the applied kinesiology procedures I had developed, I found that Anne's anxiety was affecting her stomach meridian. I had her tap beneath her eyes and concentrate on her beloved candy bars.

"On a scale of one to ten, what is your desire level now?" I asked.

"Six," she said with amazement.

We then administered the remaining treatments, and her compulsion for Snickers disappeared completely.

Anne quit eating candy bars. She began losing weight, which made both her and her cardiologist happy. The one treatment was done five years ago, and she still has no interest in Snickers.

I tried the Callahan Techniques on other patients. One, named Marie, had come to me specifically because of her weight, which was climbing out of control. This was a fairly recent problem for her. She was a successful real estate agent whose weight had ranged from 118 to 126 pounds. "I had never had a weight problem and didn't really have to worry about it," said Marie. Then anxiety crept into her life. As she tells it:

I went through a divorce and my whole life changed. I moved to San Diego and began living totally on my own. My whole family was very upset with me, my mother, my brother, and worst of all my grandparents, to whom I was very close. They all blamed me for the divorce.

While this was all going on, I was in a car accident and my cherished and irreplaceable Ferrari was totaled. The insurance company fought me on the payoff because it was considered an exotic car and had a true value that they didn't think they should have to pay.

My self-esteem was at an all-time low during this period. I became involved in a stressful and complicated romantic affair with a charming artist who turned out to be a heavy drinker and drug user.

My life began to feel very unstable and stressful. I found myself eating more often, even when I was not hungry. I was eating after I was satiated and eating more and more junk food. These compulsive eating habits continued until I weighed 153 pounds!

For the next eight years I repeatedly attempted to lose the weight. I knew all the diets and read all the latest diet books. Some of the diets worked, but only temporarily. I would always gain back the weight plus one or two pounds more. Maintaining my weight was a constant struggle. No sooner would I lose a few pounds than something stressful would happen and I would be back where I started or worse. It was frustrating and depressing.

I worked with Marie for a few hours. In that time she learned that anxiety is caused by imbalances in the electrical system; that all addicts engage in various kinds of "self-sabotage," including setting such high standards of weight loss that they automatically fail. In short, she learned everything you will learn about treating food addiction by reading this book.

Then I taught her the treatments. Here is what she had to say about the results:

The first thing I noticed was that the mental battle to not eat when I wasn't hungry was gone. It became easy to walk away from food and to avoid junk food in general. Consequently the weight dropped off because I was now eating normal amounts.

I lost eight pounds in the first two months. I then maintained that loss for about six months, when I decided I still needed to lose more to reach my desirable weight.

I practiced the Callahan Techniques to lose more weight and lost twelve pounds more. I have now maintained that weight loss for ten months. When I feel a need for comfort food, I do the techniques and the cravings go away.

Beating Chocolate

Here is another food addict whom I helped. Her name is Elizabeth and she had an addiction to chocolate. This is a common addiction in the world of the food addict, perhaps the most common except for ice cream. People undoubtedly become addicted to foods like these instead of to apples or popcorn because they carry with them the pleasure of a sugar rush. The sugar, along with their high fat content, makes them ideal comfort foods. These same factors, of course, also make them extremely fattening.

Elizabeth ate chocolate whenever she was tired, hungry, or bothered. When she was a child, Elizabeth's mother had offered her a piece of chocolate whenever anything went wrong. Chocolate, therefore, represented comfort to her. As an adult, her cravings were so strong that she avoided shopping malls, where cookie and candy stores offered irresistible temptations. "If I buy a pound, I eat a pound. If I buy five pounds, I eat five pounds. I have no control," she said.

Elizabeth had tried every diet imaginable, but she never lost weight because of her addiction to chocolate. She had even gone to a weight loss clinic that prescribed medication along with diet therapy. She told her doctor that her program had to include some chocolate or she could not stay on it. He developed a program for her that included two chocolate chip cookies per day. She went for three months but cheated. In the end she lost nine pounds. It cost her almost one thousand dollars.

"Now I am right back at it," she said. "I eat chocolate chips by the handfuls."

I explained my approach to her and then asked her to rate her desire for chocolate. Since she had just eaten some before coming in, she didn't think her desire was very high, but it quickly worked up to an eight anyway.

I had her perform the eye tap techniques and again asked her to rate her desire. "Two," she said. I gave her some written material to explain the other techniques and showed her how to use them most effectively. I put her on the same thirty-day program you will find in the back of this book.

Two months later she called and reported her success.

I have lost eight pounds because I am not eating as much chocolate as I used to. As I told my husband, "I can take it or leave it now."

I have a big package of chocolate chips in the refrigerator. [Note: A temptation that I don't recommend, but it does show how strong she is now.] The same ones I used to eat by the handful. I haven't touched them since our initial treatment. I can now go to the mall and walk right past the cookie shops, which is something I could never do before. In fact, last week I went to the mall and didn't give chocolate a thought!

There have been a couple of real tests for me. One night my husband and I went out to dinner. I ordered a chocolate mousse for dessert but I didn't eat it, didn't like it, and didn't want it. Then, a few days ago I went out looking at antiques with my husband. We passed a chocolate shop and I bought some chocolate-covered mints out of habit. I ate a couple and couldn't eat any more. I just didn't seem to need them. I handed them over to my husband, who was shocked. "I don't believe it," he said. "You never used to let me have any of these."

Balancing the System

So how do the Callahan Techniques work? And why were they successful for Anne, Marie, Elizabeth, and the hundreds of other patients I have treated?

I can answer that simply: The Callahan Techniques treat the anxiety that causes your compulsion to eat more calories than you need. Unlike traditional diet books, we won't be prescribing a specific eating program. Most of these books allow you to keep overeating by substituting foods like carrots and cauliflower for real weight-gainers like chocolate and ice cream. They ignore anxiety, allowing it to build, which eventually leads you back to the rich and fattening foods that do cause weight gain. They are simply replacing one tranquilizer with another, the way heroin addicts switch to methadone to "cure" their heroin addiction. Methadone is just another form of addiction that tranquilizes anxiety. Like drug addicts who return to heroin, virtually all food addicts will eventually go back to the rich and fattening foods that mask anxiety the best.

The Callahan Techniques don't cause you to substitute one addiction for another. Instead they address and eliminate the anxiety that causes your food cravings. They do this by correcting the cause of anxiety where it first occurs, in the body's energy system. The energy system is the first system in the body to respond to any sort of stress, whether physical or mental. This response by the energy system always leads to physical consequences in the body. To prove my point, let's look at two common mental states, happiness and anger.

When you are happy and laughing, the body releases chemicals known as endorphins that make you feel good. These naturally occurring substances are approximately thirty times more potent than an equal amount of morphine. They give you that "natural high" you feel after watching a good comedy or laughing with good friends. They relax you and make you feel good.

Anger is the opposite mental state. It can be caused by many situations, from a traffic jam to an argument. First you feel a rise in anger at the situation. You then experience a release of adrenaline that causes your arteries to constrict and produce physical symptoms such as increased pulse rate, elevated blood pressure, sweaty palms, and maybe clenched fists.

This is how the body's chemical system responds to two common mental states. It responds in similar ways to a variety of common mental states such as depression, boredom, anxiety, fear, and so on.

But the body doesn't respond in only chemical or physical ways. It responds electrically, too. In fact, where mood states are concerned, I believe it responds electrically *first,* chemically *second,* physically *third,* and psychologically *last.*

This has been demonstrated many times in the medical research on the body's fascinating energy system.

I will discuss some of this research in Chapter 5. But for now, consider that it is the energy system that causes your anxiety level to rise. A rush of adrenaline may be the result, but the primary cause of the food addict's anxiety is an energy imbalance.

Interestingly enough, any mood state can cause a rise in anxiety that leads to eating when you're not hungry. I have patients who overeat only when they are happy as well as patients who overeat only when they are sad. Sometimes patients can't pinpoint when their food cravings begin, but they need something to help them "calm down."

The fact is that anything causing an imbalance in the body's energy system can lead to anxiety and thus to the refrigerator. If the source of that imbalance is corrected, so is the obsessive need to eat.

The Callahan Techniques work by balancing and realigning the body's energy system. I believe these electrical circuits are prone to go out of alignment in some people. Sometimes the cause is internal and sometimes it is precipitated by external events, but whatever the cause, anxiety leads to compulsive eating.

New and "Unusual"

The Callahan Techniques are different from conventional (or any other) psychotherapies. Most people who go to a psychologist for treatment of eating disorders want and expect hour-long sessions during which they sit in a chair or lie on a couch and talk about their problems.

They expect to be able to blame "something in their past" for the way they are now. Perhaps a mother who constantly urged them to eat. A need to gain weight in order to avoid intimacy. Anything that will take the focus off them and their addiction.

The Callahan Techniques treat the anxiety that causes food addiction.

Many people want to sit in group therapy sessions with other food addicts and talk about their never-ending battles with food. The Callahan Techniques are done by yourself, when you need them. You don't need to talk about the food fight with anyone else because you can win it on your own, often in a matter of minutes.

Perhaps it is the simplicity of this treatment that makes some patients and psychologists skeptical. After all, any kind of rapid treatment is regarded with skepticism in the psychological world. Psychotherapy usually involves hours of therapy over months of time. The ease of these treatments leads some to dismiss the Callahan Techniques as simply the power of suggestion. "If people believe it, then it works," said one cynical psychologist.

The Callahan Techniques work whether people believe in them or not. Most of the people I treat are skeptics. Because of this, I don't get my fair share of placebo cures, but, of course, I really don't need them. One advantage in treating skeptics is that it proves that the techniques work regardless of mind-set. I compare the Callahan Techniques to the treatment of an infection with antibiotics, because they work whether you believe in them or not.

Living with Food

The Callahan Techniques will help you abstain from food. But they will also help you live *with* food. After all, there are few legal acts that exceed the pleasure of eating. It is when you are unable to stop eating even though you aren't actually hungry that food is an addiction.

My techniques let you eat what you want without eating too much. They help you to live rationally.

The Callahan Techniques make living on a balanced diet much easier for the food-addicted because they show you how to:

- Keep from binge eating.

- Relieve anxiety, which is the real force behind food addiction.

- Get rid of addictive urges.

- Eliminate the toughest problem of all, which I call "psychological reversal" and which causes that tendency in almost all food addicts to "fall off the wagon," regain the weight, and sabotage their own best efforts.

Best of all, the Callahan Techniques will give you control over your appetite and help you discover new pleasure in reasonable eating.

T W O

Why Do I Eat When I'm Not Hungry?

"Why do I eat when I'm not hungry?"

Searching for the answer to that question is what led you to this book. You have probably tried many diets to get the weight off, and maybe even some behavior modification programs to change your eating habits, but they haven't worked. Soon you are again eating when you aren't hungry and wondering why. No matter what you try, the weight creeps back.

I am going to tell you why in one word. *Anxiety.* For reasons you never knew before reading this book, you are plagued with anxiety.

Anxiety is the presence of fear when there is no objective reason to be afraid. That doesn't necessarily mean you are experiencing anxiety for no real reason. There is always a reason. You may be anxious about how you think other people are perceiving you. You may be anxious about stresses in your life such as the amount of work you have to do or some problem in the family. You may even be able to point out reasons for your high anxiety level. But your anxiety is out of proportion to the reason. Oftentimes, these "reasons" aren't the reason people are anxious at all. They are merely used as explanations.

For example, I asked one of my patients why she was always so anxious. Her answer was that work was stressful. Work is stressful for many people, and can certainly be a source of anxiety. But then I asked her when she did most of her overeating. She said she did it on weekends, the days when she didn't have to go to work!

When she realized the illogic of what she had said, she realized that there was more to her anxiety than just work. She was having anxiety attacks that were caused by an internal source, not something from outside. Yet she was latching onto work as the source of all of her anxiety. In reality it was caused by her energy system being out of balance. But in her attempt to explain the problem, she blamed it all on work.

In many ways the anxiety that makes you eat when you aren't hungry can be compared to the anxiety that causes phobias. To refresh your memory, a phobia is an unrealistic fear. That causes vague or persistent anxiety.

For instance, the most common phobia is stage fright, the fear of performing or speaking in front of an audience. Other common phobias are fear of heights, flying, doctors, dentists, needles, animals, bugs, closed spaces—the list goes on and on. People with phobias have anxiety tied to a specific source.

Why the energy system goes out of balance and causes phobias is a mystery. But that doesn't mean that some psychologists haven't tried to explain why they happen. For instance, Freud developed the theory that a phobia is a "protective" mental affliction that keeps its victim from facing the far more painful knowledge that his father would like to castrate him.

Students of Freud tried to substantiate this theory by searching through the childhood memories of phobic patients in hopes of relocating that critical moment when a specific fear first developed.

Besides the fact that this theory didn't take women into consideration, it had other flaws that soon became evident to the researchers. Most phobics remember their first phobic attacks. They had nothing to do with a fear that their father would castrate them. They were always tied to something else, usually a source that was a mystery. Nonetheless, treatment proceeded on the basis of the castration theory. It was quite ineffective.

Other Attempts at Treatment

Many other psychological treatments have been used in an attempt to quell the anxiety that causes phobias. I want to mention them here because they are the same therapies used with a high rate of failure in the treatment of food addiction. As you read through these remember that the Callahan Techniques have a cure rate for simple phobias of over *95 percent* in just a few minutes! All the traditional treatments require many hours of therapy and have "success" rates that are abysmally low. You rarely hear anyone talk about cure.

The reason for the difference? I treat the actual cause of the problem while others simply treat the symptoms.

Behavior Therapy

This type of therapy is designed to alter a patient's response to a situation. Behavior therapists take many different approaches, but all play off the idea that if a person is relaxed, his response to certain things will be different. This is something like easing into cold water. If it is done slowly enough, it really doesn't feel so bad.

For example, a child who fears rabbits may be given a piece of candy. While he is eating, a toy bunny is brought into the room but kept as far away from the child as possible. The child is made aware of the bunny, but no threat is made to bring the toy closer. Each time the child is brought in for treatment, more candy is given and the bunny is moved closer. If the fear is not severe, the child may begin to associate the bunny with the candy, not the fear that it once caused.

Similar behavior therapy has been used to get people to stop eating when they aren't hungry. One technique has a person chew a mouthful of cookies and then open his mouth and show the moist contents to another person, who is also attempting to break the eating addiction.

The theory is that the sight of these mushed-up cookies will break a person of wanting to eat them. It usually just makes him chew with his mouth shut.

Behavior therapy is probably the most commonly used approach in food addiction programs. There are a number of other techniques used by behavior therapists to get the eater's mind off food, including timers and rubber bands around the wrist to be snapped when the eater gets hungry. Relaxation techniques are also used in behavior therapy to get a person's mind off food.

As you can imagine, such treatment takes many hours, usually costs a lot of money, and is generally not very successful when it comes to stopping food addiction.

Clinical Hypnosis

Hypnosis has been used for many years to treat phobias and overeating. The exact nature of the hypnotic state is not totally understood, but it is believed that a person who is hypnotized goes into a state known as hypnogogia in which he appears to be asleep but is actually very aware.

Patients being treated for phobias or food addiction might be given a positive suggestion while under hypnosis. A person who fears heights might be told, for example, that he is climbing a mountain, enjoys the scenery, and feels fine. When he is brought out of his hypnotic trance, he will be reminded of how wonderful he felt on his "climb."

Similarly, a food addict, after being put into a state of hypnosis, might be taken on a guided tour of a buffet filled with all the foods he desires. But rather than being allowed to gorge himself, he will take great pride in being able to pass through the room without eating anything. When he is brought out of his hypnotic trance, he will be reminded how wonderful it felt to be able to pass through a room full of tasty delights and not touch a thing.

This approach works only for a small number of patients.

Rational Emotive Therapy

I am particularly familiar with this type of therapy because I used to help train other therapists in this approach. I even used it with helpful results in my own life.

Rational emotive therapy is done through repetitive exposure to the fear-producing situation during which the patient repeatedly reminds himself that his fear is irrational. The theory here is that the individual has certain thoughts that cause particular emotions. When the emotions do not coincide with reality, the individual's beliefs are considered irrational. An active process of challenging the thoughts and irrational beliefs is encouraged.

A therapist might attempt rational emotive therapy with a food addict by having him confront foods he commonly eats when he isn't hungry while repeatedly telling himself that he really doesn't need the food. The patient would challenge and attack the irrational belief that he must eat.

The Anxiety Allergy Analogy

Anxiety causes your food addiction just as it causes the irrational fear of phobics. However, there is one important difference: Where a phobic can point to something specific as the source of his anxiety (fear of bridges, for instance), the food addict's anxiety is usually not that specific. You may not even be conscious of having anxiety.

These anxiety attacks are like allergic responses, in which the body has an irrational response to a harmless substance. This is an important concept for understanding the Callahan Techniques, so let me explain it in depth.

One of the ways the body defends itself against invading organisms is by producing substances known as histamines. These substances work by engulfing the invaders and passing them out of the body through channels like the nose and mouth. That is why infections such as a cold or the flu are accompanied by a runny nose, swollen sinus tissues, and excessive tearing.

When the body defends itself in this manner against a real invader like the flu, the response is appropriate. But sometimes the body defends itself against a nonthreat such as pollen or even dust. When this happens and histamines from the body's defending cells cause swollen sinus tissues and an abundance of mucus, this is called an allergic reaction or an allergy. The body is defending against a non-threat.

In the same way, a phobia or chronic anxiety is an important defense system gone awry. In chronic anxiety, the alarm is going off at all times and it is a false alarm. It is just as painful, however, to the victim as if he were in real danger. It is a horrible experience, made worse by the knowledge that the emotion makes no sense. Seeking relief, these people turn to addictions for help. The only difficulty is that the addiction usually creates worse problems than the original one.

Some anxiety is good and appropriate. But food addiction is caused by anxiety gone haywire. A person either feels far more anxious in a situation than he should or he feels anxious for no reason at all. When this happens, he is experiencing an anxiety attack.

For instance, the fear and anxiety felt by a woman walking alone on a deserted street at night is appropriate, because it keeps her alert and ready to defend herself. The same is true of the fear and anxiety felt by a soldier in combat. Without that heightened awareness caused by a very real fear of death, the soldier might not respond as quickly to an attacker.

This response is known in medicine as the "fight or flight" response. It is the way the body prepares itself to respond to an emergency. At the onset of fear, adrenaline is pumped into the bloodstream, causing muscles to become tense, heart rate and breathing to speed up.

When the fear is appropriate this response is fine. After all, it is intended as protection against a life-threatening situation. But sometimes this anxiety comes on like an allergy—for no reason at all.

A person with allergies doesn't cure his problem with antihistamines, and you don't cure your anxiety with the intake of food. What you do is temporarily mask the problem. When the tranquilizing effects of the food wear off, the anxiety will be back, often building and worsening over time.

Addiction to Tranquilizers

The evidence of my work strongly suggests that all addictions are addictions to tranquilizers. Whether you are addicted to food, alcohol, drugs, cigarettes, gambling, sex, or biting your fingernails, you are addicted to something that will mask your anxiety.

These tranquilizers don't cure the anxiety, they just mask it. You know that. You know that the anxiety that leads you to overeat makes no sense. You know that you feel bad and even stupid for having this anxiety, but there seems to be nothing you can do but eat to gain relief from it. That is why you eat when you aren't hungry. Even though you really don't want to eat, you have learned to do it to mask the anxiety that is often felt in the pit of your stomach.

Soon you find you are addicted to food.

Addictions are probably the most misunderstood of all psychological problems. Even the word itself is frequently used inappropriately. For example, a person who reads a lot is said to be "addicted to reading." People who train for marathons are said to be "running addicts."

These people are not addicts.

For someone to be an addict, he has to have a dependency on some substance or activity that causes harm and interference in his life. As a food addict you depend on food to tranquilize yourself. Without it you are uncomfortable. But your reliance on this tranquilizer interferes with your life. After all, you are overweight, or not getting proper nutrition from fad diets, either of which hinders long-term health as well as day-to-day living.

As a food addict, you are caught in a terrible cycle. You want to stop eating when you aren't hungry. But without food the anxiety is never covered up. It builds and builds until it forces you to deal with it the only way you know how—by eating.

The Pathway to Addiction

How does food addiction start? Let me tell you about one of my patients:

As a child, Cheryl came home from nursery school frightened by having been away from home and the security of her mother for the first time. Many kids are nervous on the first day of school, but Cheryl tended to be more nervous than most kids. When she came home, her mother was in the kitchen baking a cake.

Cheryl didn't say anything but her mother took one look at her and knew she was more upset than usual. She knew Cheryl had eaten a good lunch before leaving school. However, from her own experience she knew the comforting feeling that comes from nice-tasting food. "Here, darling," her mother said. "Let me fix you a piece of cake. I know it will make you feel better."

Now, as an adult, Cheryl sees food as comfort, a means of reducing her anxiety.

This is an experience most children—and mothers—can identify with. Not every child who is given food as comfort will become a food addict. That will depend on *how anxious the individual is* and *how effective the food is* at masking the anxiety. The more effective the food, the more likely it is to be used again and again.

All addictions begin as psychological addictions. This means that there is a need in the mind to tranquilize some anxiety. Many addictions go on to become physiological, which means that the body actually needs the substance that masks the anxiety. Remember, every alcoholic, every heroin addict, every smoker, every thumb-sucker, every nail-biter, every substance-abuser or person engaging in compulsive behavior is suffering from anxiety.

A prime example of a commonly used drug that is thought to be physiologically addicting is nicotine in the form of cigarettes. The surgeon general called this the number-one addiction in America and compared it to heroin in the way it creates physical need.

Cigarettes do create a physical need. However, the physiological aspects of nicotine addiction is over within about three days of abstinence. Does that mean the psychological need for this substance is gone? Certainly not. After three days of abstinence, the physiological aspects of the addiction are over. Yet the smoker still suffers terrible desire for a cigarette for months or years after quitting. This is because the anxiety that created the addiction to begin with continues untreated after the physiological addiction is gone. What we call "withdrawal" is actually anxiety.

Tranquilizers only mask anxiety, they don't get rid of it. If you don't believe me, try this simple experiment: Next time you have the desire to eat when you aren't hungry, don't do it. Try to keep yourself busy with other things. Try not to think about eating. Try.

If you are truly a food addict you will be aware of a growing craving, which you may be able to relate to anxiety-producing situations. You will be overwhelmed by anxiety in just the same way that a smoker is overwhelmed by his craving for a cigarette at times when he can't have one.

The addict who is withdrawn from his tranquilizer will become aware of the anxiety that is the root cause of his addiction. That anxiety doesn't go away on its own. Without treatment to eliminate the anxiety, it just lingers on and on. Which is why people lose tremendous amounts of weight only to gain it back in a relatively short period of time. Like a weed that eventually pushes through a cement sidewalk, untreated anxiety forces itself through a person's willpower. That is why so many of the "great" diet programs have such high failure rates—they don't treat anxiety.

We Treat Anxiety,
the Cause of Addiction

The Callahan Techniques for treating food addiction are successful because they *do* treat anxiety. We don't advocate a certain type of diet, or recommend that you drink a certain amount of water or "count" your food the way diet programs do.

We don't do that because the Callahan Techniques aren't a diet. They are an inexpensive, natural, rapid, and comprehensive way of treating the anxiety that makes you crave food and overeat. They treat the basic cause of your problem.

THREE

Psychological Reversal

Have you ever been around someone who is especially hostile, negative, and nasty for no obvious reason? Or, to make the question a little more personal: Have *you* ever been hostile, negative, and nasty for no real reason? I am sure the answer to both those questions is "yes."

At times we all become aware that we are behaving in a destructive and hurtful way toward people we love, and yet we seem helpless to stop behaving that way. It is almost as if our willpower is suspended and we seem unable to do anything about it. At such times we are what I call psychologically reversed.

That same helpless feeling of suspended willpower can come over you as a food addict. You truly want to lose weight and quit eating so much. But despite your best intentions and against your will, you often cannot keep from eating when you are not hungry. Why is this happening? It is happening because you are psychologically reversed.

When you are psychologically reversed, your actions are contrary to what you say you want to do. You might say that you want to quit eating when you aren't hungry, and in your heart of hearts you really do want to quit overeating. But in reality you are continuing to overeat. You are sabotaging your own efforts, you feel helpless and you don't know why.

Psychological reversal creates a condition in which your motivation operates in a way that is directly opposed to the way it should work. You should be able to plan to lose weight and then accomplish it in a rational and logical fashion. But that isn't what happens. People who are psychologically reversed imagine losing weight and then something inside them sabotages their every effort. With psychological reversal, a person feels stressed when he just thinks of getting better.

Let me give you an example of a person who is psychologically reversed:

Jim is a very successful stockbroker. He is hardworking, disciplined, diligent, responsible, and an outstanding performer in every area of his life. He has a great marriage, many good friends, and a fine social life.

Only one thing bothered Jim: He could not lose that twenty extra pounds no matter what he tried. And he tried a lot. He was physically active and went on several different diet programs. But within months of losing the desired amount of weight, Jim gained it all back.

When he approached me for help, I decided to examine his surroundings. I visited his office and found that he kept a candy dish loaded with fattening goodies on the corner of his desk. He said that the candy was for his clients, but he admitted that he munched on it all day long, too.

In all other areas of his life Jim was disciplined. Yet here at the office, he kept "candy for clients" right under his nose. He was sabotaging himself by keeping the stuff right there. He was psychologically reversed on losing weight. The candy was there to help him betray his own efforts.

I treated Jim with the techniques you will find in Part II. I showed him how to fix his reversal. He got rid of the candy dish that day. He has now actually done what he just said he wanted to do all along—lose weight and keep it off.

The Roots of Reversal

Many psychologists have stated over the years that certain patients want to die, want to be ill, or want to be disturbed even though they say they want to get better. Freud called this a "death instinct." And psychologist Albert Ellis stated that all neurotics are "self-defeating" in their efforts to get well.

Psychological reversal explains and makes sense of these two concepts. Psychological reversal is a state of the body and the mind that blocks the natural healing (energy) force within and prevents effective therapeutic intervention. People don't usually want to hurt themselves. I believe there is a block inside the body and mind that keeps people from achieving certain goals. The goal food addicts have failed to achieve is avoiding too much food. For others the goal might be avoiding too much alcohol or giving up cigarettes. Addictions come in many forms, but their cause is always a rise in anxiety that needs to be masked.

Dr. David Walther discussed my concept of psychological reversal in his recent book *Applied Kinesiology: Synopsis.* "Most practicing physicians can recognize psychologically reversed individuals in their practices. These are often the individuals who respond poorly to treatment; when there is some improvement in a condition, they will dwell on the negative aspects. Even when the improvement is pointed out, they will immediately change the subject back to the negative aspects."

This blockage sustains negative attitudes and prevents the success of any therapy, no matter what the form of therapy is. For some reason, your motivation has been turned upside down. You work against yourself and you are stressed when you imagine getting better. For any therapy to work, the psychological reversal must first be undone.

A good analogy for the way psychological reversal affects us is to imagine a series of train engines hooked together and controlled by one engineer. His engine is pointed south, which is the way he wants to go. The other engines are all heading north. The more he increases the power, the faster all the engines head north. Since they are pointed the wrong way, there is little he can do but be dragged along in frustration.

Is psychological reversal uncommon? No. Psychological reversals, or blocks to healing or treatment, can and do occur in all areas of living. When I was a student I was blocked in algebra, for example. I grasped other subjects with ease, but when it came to algebra my mind turned to mush and I just couldn't get it no matter how many hours of study I put in. People are reversed on being successful in their careers, their love lives, and in any other area you can imagine.

Going by the number of books on love which could have the collective title *Why Do I Always Pick a Rat for a Lover?*, psychological reversal in the realm of romantic love is practically of plague proportions.

Over 90 percent of the American population has difficulty losing weight, and most of these people are psychologically reversed. They want to lose excess pounds but they just can't because they are sabotaging themselves without even knowing it.

Discovering Reversal

I discovered the concept of psychological reversal while working with an overweight woman who wanted to be thin. She had been dieting unsuccessfully for years. Yet despite her failure to cut down on eating, she insisted that she wanted to lose weight.

Using a muscle test I had adapted from applied kinesiology, I asked her to imagine herself the way she wanted to be. The results startled me. When she pictured herself minus the extra weight, it stressed her, causing her to test weak.

We were both surprised. Yet despite the negative results, she insisted that she did want to lose weight.

I tried a different approach. "Picture yourself thirty pounds heavier than you are," I suggested. The thought invigorated rather than stressed her. Now she tested strong.

I then had her say, "I want to lose weight." The test revealed that her statement was not true. Somewhere deep inside, she did *not* want to lose weight.

I then had her say, "I want to gain weight." This time she tested strong.

Clearly there was a discrepancy between what she said she wanted and what the tests showed.

I tried this test on six other clients who had been dieting for months or years without success. They showed the same pattern. They *said* they wanted to lose weight. But when I tested them, I found that they really didn't want to lose weight. They were *reversed* on eating less.

This was not the first time I had found resistance to treatment. But now I had a tool with which to identify it and possibly to overcome it. I called this condition psychological reversal.

I first thought this weakness in my overweight patients was associated with a fear of sexuality. It is often assumed by psychologists that people become overweight to "shield" themselves against sex.

But when I discovered the same psychological reversal in a big, tough, happily married construction foreman, I had to rethink that supposition. I knew this man well, I knew that he had no fear of sex, and certainly no fear of being slender and sexually attractive. So why were people who said they truly wanted to lose weight unable to do so?

I began to test my other clients in regard to their major psychological problems. I wanted to see if they were reversed, too. They had come to me for a variety of problems: "I want to get over my anxiety attacks." "I want to have a better relationship with my wife." "I want to overcome my frigidity." "I want to be successful." "I want to become a better actor."

I asked them to make a statement that was the reverse of why they came and then administered the test. I was flabbergasted at the results. All of my difficult patients got weak when they thought of getting better. This indicated that deep down they really didn't want to get better. The patients who came to me for anxiety attacks and who were not responding to treatment, tested strong when they said, "I *don't* want to get over my anxiety attacks." Some of the men who came to me because their marriages were disintegrating tested stronger when they said, "I *don't* want to have a better relationship with my wife." These patients got weaker at the thought of getting better.

No wonder psychotherapy is so difficult! Psychological reversal makes people do things they don't want to do!

I looked back on former patients and realized that many difficult patients I had treated in the past fit neatly into this category of being psychologically reversed. They were patients for whom treatment had been a struggle, patients who constantly voiced their desire to get better but who failed miserably in their attempts to make the necessary changes.

I believed them when they said they wanted to get better. More important, *they* believed themselves when they said they wanted to get better. The problem was that something deep inside kept them from carrying out their stated goals. They were psychologically reversed, or *blocked,* on getting better.

Psychological reversal comes in many forms. Comedian Flip Wilson verbalized it in one of his comedy routines. Whenever the character he was portraying did something wrong, he declared, "The devil made me do it."

Even St. Paul said, "The devil made me do it" when he found himself backsliding in his faith. In chapter 7, verses 18 and 19 of Romans, Paul said: "For I know that in me dwelleth no good thing: for to will is present with me; but how to perform that which is good I find not.

"For the good that I would I do not: but the evil which I would not, that I do."

The term "self-defeating" or "self-destructive" used by frustrated therapists to describe certain patients is actually an expression for the self-sabotage generated by psychological reversal.

Addicted gamblers, for example, are psychologically reversed on their problem. They may say they want to stop gambling and may even stop for a short period of time. But soon they are back at the tables, gambling.

As a food addict, your psychological reversal can take a number of forms. You may want to lose ten or fifteen pounds and, though you never seem to add more weight, you just can't get rid of that extra baggage. Or you may want to lose considerably more weight than that but find it impossible because "something" inside won't let you stop eating when you aren't hungry.

I have learned that what people *do* tells me much more about what they believe than what they *say*. If you want to know if you are psychologically reversed, see if what you *do* agrees with what you *say* you want to do. If your actions are contrary to your stated goals, then you probably have what I call psychological reversal. You are turned against yourself and your own interests.

The Degrees of Reversal

Since identifying psychological reversal, I have had the opportunity to work with the condition in all of its forms with thousands of patients.

Some of the patients I work with are *massively* reversed. That means their lives are fraught with internal roadblocks. They are self-sabotaging in almost every respect. In almost anything they say they want to accomplish—from weight loss and curing food addiction to improving love and interpersonal relationships—psychological reversal keeps them from attaining their goals.

Having worked with psychological reversal for so many years, I can sometimes detect massive reversal in a patient's manner, facial expression, attitude, or verbal responses. Obvious expressions of psychological reversal are outright hostility, negativism, sarcasm, or hopelessness, which are pervasive and chronically present.

These attitudes reflect the fact that any form of psychological reversal is rooted in a deep rejection of self. Reversed people do not believe they deserve to succeed. They consider themselves unworthy of good things and deserving of failure and unhappiness.

Dr. Albert Ellis colorfully dubbed this the "worthless piece of shit" syndrome. He believed that a person suffering from this condition considered himself so valueless that he deserved no happiness or success in life. These people were *reversed* on anything good or desirable in their lives.

For most of us psychological reversal is limited to specific areas of life. For instance, as a food addict, you may be successful in every aspect of your life except being able to stop eating when you aren't hungry.

A patient named Diane is an example of a high achiever with just such a specific reversal. Here, in her own words, is her story:

I am a vice president of a major real estate company in the Southwest. I was under thirty when I got to that position, which surprised everyone since no woman who was that young had ever reached such a position at this company.

It didn't surprise me that I reached VP, since I have always been able to reach any goal that I set my mind to. When I decided to get my master's degree in one year I got organized and did it. When I decided to become the top salesperson at my company, I just knuckled down and did it.

That is the most frustrating thing to me about my eating. No matter how much I knuckle down, I can't seem to stop eating so much. I promise myself that I'm going to lose weight, but something inside of me just keeps me eating.

It is frustrating, because my eating habits are the only thing in my life that I can't control.

In Diane, we have a person who is specifically reversed about eating. Notice that she is happy with the control she has over the rest of her life. Yet this lack of control over her eating habits has her baffled. When she asked me, "Why do I eat when I am not hungry?" my answer was simple enough: "It's because you can't do what you want to do. You are psychologically reversed on eating."

A Boon to Treatment

The discovery of psychological reversal and how to deal with it was a great boon to treatment. In the past I had spent hours, weeks, months, and even years trying to overcome a patient's negativism. But since discovering psychological reversal and how to correct it, I have been able to improve my success in reducing addictive urges to better than 95 percent. Before discovering psychological reversal, the success rate was 45 percent.

I treat reversal in my patients by promoting self-acceptance and "embedding" it in them with the Callahan Techniques for treating psychological reversal.

This is truly a mixture of traditional treatment with a new and powerful technique. Virtually all psychotherapists promote self-acceptance in their clients. They have found that people who denigrate themselves because of their problems have even greater difficulty overcoming those problems.

As a psychotherapist with a traditional background, I used self-acceptance as a way to help overcome psychological reversal and to support the physical treatment. To my pleasant surprise, I found that uttering a statement of self-acceptance *("I profoundly and completely accept myself with all my problems and all my shortcomings")* would temporarily correct the reversal problem. I also found that by uttering a self-denigrating statement, an *un*reversed patient would become reversed.

Although a statement of self-acceptance temporarily corrects psychological reversal, I found that combining this affirmation with a direct treatment to the energy system resulted in an even better correction.

The basic treatment for psychological reversal involves repeating the self-affirmation *("I profoundly and completely accept myself with all my problems and all my shortcomings")* while using two or three fingers to tap the reversal treatment spot on the outside of the opposite hand. See the illustration on the following page.

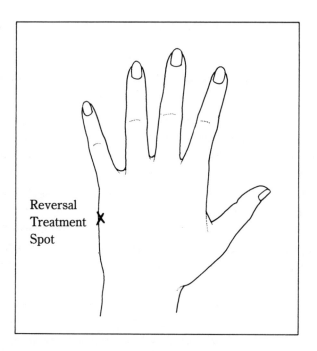

Reversal
Treatment
Spot

By following this procedure, psychological reversal can be corrected and treatment for food addiction can begin.

An Inner Imbalance

Psychological reversal, like other problems, is a condition resulting from an imbalance in the body's electrical system, over which a person has little control. As I have said, a psychologically reversed person is not deliberately trying to be self-destructive.

Treatments for psychological reversal have been used successfully to cure a wide variety of psychological and medical problems. For instance, Dr. Robert Blaich, who specializes in treating world-class athletes, has helped his patients improve performance by treating them for psychological reversal. This doesn't surprise me, since the real differences in performance among most world-class athletes are due to psychological factors. One of the consequences of psychological reversal is that it affects the neurological organization, which in turn affects timing, coordination, and concentration, all of which are important factors in achieving that extra edge the world-class athlete must have to be a winner.

In one study conducted by Dr. Blaich, reading speed and comprehension were improved in an experimental group of people being treated for reversal. The Callahan Techniques improved reading speed and comprehension in a group of professionals much better than more time-consuming procedures requiring specialized training to perform.

We also have anecdotal evidence that psychological reversal prevents natural healing of physical problems. Here is an example taken from a letter written by Dr. John Hughes of Ashland, Kentucky:

I was teaching a class for doctors and wanted to demonstrate psychological reversal for the class. I called for a volunteer and the wife of one of the doctors came forward.

The subject reported having a root canal performed on one of her teeth and she had developed a hole in her lower right jaw. This had continued to produce an exudate [discharge] for about a year and a half. She had consulted another dentist but the condition continued. This treatment occurred on a weekend and I saw the doctor and his wife the following Thursday at a meeting.

The doctor said, "I want to tell you what happened to my wife after you corrected her psychological reversal. That evening the hole in her jaw really started to run and produce more discharge than ever before. Then it just stopped."

They had a dentist examine the area and he said all the tissue appeared clear and healthy.

I saw the couple a few months later and she said, "Do you want to see my scar?" It was totally healed.

I am aware that this, as well as other incidents of physical healing after treatment for psychological reversal, might be simple coincidence. But I bring it up here because these events are so commonplace in my practice, and because I believe the physical effects of psychological reversal are fertile ground for further research.

As far as food addiction goes, the discovery of psychological reversal can relieve unsuccessful dieters from a tremendous amount of undeserved guilt. Now they know they are not trying to hurt themselves! They are victims of an energy imbalance that keeps their anxiety level unbearably high.

"Self-Defeating" Traits

There are eight traits for "self-defeating personality disorder" that have been proposed for listing in the standard diagnostic manual used by psychotherapists. Although they are not yet listed, I mention them here because they appear to relate closely to what I call psychological reversal.

For it to be assumed that you have a self-defeating personality disorder, you would have to rate yourself high in six of the eight traits. To do so would qualify you as what I call a "massively reversed person," one who is incapable of doing many things you say you want to do, including lose weight. With anywhere from one to six traits you are still psychologically reversed, but perhaps to a lesser degree.

Here are the traits:

- Chooses persons or situations that lead to his or her disappointment, failure, or mistreatment. Even when better options are clearly available to him or her.

- Rejects or renders ineffective the attempts of others to help him or her.

- Following positive personal events (for example: a new achievement) responds with depression, guilt, or behavior that brings about pain.

- Incites angry or rejecting responses from others and then feels hurt, defeated, or humiliated. For example: criticizes spouse in public, provoking an angry counterattack, and then feels devastated.

- Turns down opportunities for pleasure and is reluctant to acknowledge enjoying himself or herself despite having adequate social skills and the capacity for pleasure.

- Fails to accomplish tasks crucial for his or her personal objectives despite demonstrated ability to do so.

For example: helps fellow students write papers but is unable to write his or her own.

- Is bored with or uninterested in people who consistently treat him or her well. For example: is unattracted to caring sexual partners.

- Engages in excessive self-sacrifice that is unsolicited and discouraged by the intended recipients of the sacrifice.

You can certainly see how these eight traits describe a self-defeating person. But a person doesn't have to be massively reversed to block effective treatment. Most psychological reversals are "limited" or specialized, which means you are blocked in only certain specific areas of your life.

If you can identify with even one of these traits, you are still reversed but to a lesser degree. Don't feel bad, though. Most people are reversed to one degree or another. The good news is that the Callahan Techniques provide a treatment that can correct this problem.

The Most Important Concept

Understanding psychological reversal is important in overcoming your food addiction. You simply cannot lose weight or keep it off until you correct the reversal problem.

Why? Because psychological reversal creates a block against achieving your goals. Until that block is removed, you will not be able to stop eating when you are not hungry.

Why are so many food (and other) addicts reversed? I believe that there is something in the very nature of masking anxiety that leads to reversal, or a "block" against healing. It is this block against healing that makes addictions so difficult to treat.

FOUR

Why the Callahan Techniques Work

Most of us love bells and whistles. We are often impressed by complicated therapies with big names, psychologists with theories that are difficult to understand, and treatments that are intricate, take a long time, yet may help very few people.

There are many such therapies in psychology, ones that I consider "somewhat credible" because they offer some small relief from problems like food addiction. These therapies—behavior therapy such as systematic desensitization and rational emotive psychotherapy, for example—show marginal improvement in patients who are treated with them. None of them has shown great success in the treatment of food addiction.

But they do have bells and whistles. And of course they all take a lot of time.

An example of one such therapeutic approach is the form of behavior therapy known as systematic desensitization. This therapy is based on the logical and systematic confrontation of a series of fears. Together the patient and therapist rank the patient's fears in order of severity. Those that produce the greatest anxiety are put at the top of the list, those that produce the least anxiety are at the bottom.

Then, in a very relaxed condition, which might be achieved by hypnosis or developed relaxation, the patient may be helped to visualize these stressful situations, beginning with those that are lowest on his list. That way the least fearful situations are the first to be confronted and overcome. With each session the patient confronts fears higher up on the scale.

Systematic desensitization takes an average of twenty-five to thirty hourly sessions, which makes it quite expensive. Its success rate is very low, but it fits the image of what many people think psychotherapy should be because it takes a lot of time and involves hands-on work by a therapist.

No Bells and Whistles, Just Results

I mention bells and whistles here because the Callahan Techniques have none. They are quick and easy treatments that take only minutes and get very rapid results. They aren't expensive. They aren't time-consuming . . .

. . . And they are effective. They are quick and powerful treatments for food addiction (and many other psychological problems) with a high success rate.

The speed with which I treat food addiction has given me problems over the years. Most psychotherapists are prejudiced against any treatment they consider a "quick fix." They relate the quick fix to something like plugging a hole in a water pipe with chewing gum: It will get temporary results, but the hole will never be truly mended. Recent research, nevertheless, suggests that a quick fix is the best way to treat behaviorial problems. A scientific paper published in *Behaviour Research & Therapy* reported that the patients who responded quickest to phobia therapy experienced less recurrence of their fears over time than did the "slower responders."

Still, psychotherapists are trained to believe that psychological problems such as food addiction take a long time to treat. And even then, they don't expect much success.

The reason they don't have much success is that they are treating the symptoms, not the cause of food addiction. *You can't overcome a psychological problem by treating its symptoms.* That is like putting a cold towel on the head of a person with a foot infection. The fever may subside, but it will come back if the infection itself isn't treated and cleared up.

When the cause of a problem is not known there is generally a great diversity of treatments and controversy surrounding them. For example, before the cause of tuberculosis was found, there were many different kinds of competing treatments, all of them very involved. That is the state of psychology today. There are all kinds of theories and practices and none is striking for its success in curing psychological problems.

Once the basic cause of a problem is discovered, the treatment and the cure often become simple and effective. The ease and effectiveness of my treatments reflect the fact that I have found the basic cause of these problems.

Anxiety and Its Cause

The Callahan Techniques are different from any other treatment for food addiction. I believe that anxiety is the *root* cause of food and other addictions. Other therapies may not treat anxiety at all, or may treat it only as a symptom of other problems, such as job stress or marital disharmony. They ignore the cause of the food addiction, which is the need to tranquilize that powerful anxiety with food. Instead they treat the problem in a backward fashion. They go in search of something causing stress or frustration in the person's life. Granted, these things are sometimes easy to find. After all, most people have *some* source of dissatisfaction in their lives.

But sometimes these problems just don't exist. Sometimes people are addicted to food because they have general, pervasive anxiety and food is an effective *masker* of anxiety. This presents a dilemma for traditional therapists, who don't know that anxiety is the cause of food addiction and who need some kind of tangible "demon" they can fight. But in many people these demons don't exist.

Since most therapists don't know that anxiety is the cause, they continue to search for a "reason" people eat when they aren't hungry. It's this search for reasons that leads to such explanations as: "People overeat because they want to shield themselves from the world around them." Or, "Women overeat because they fear sexual intimacy."

There are many "reasons" given by therapists for overeating. But most of these "reasons" are wrong, or merely symptoms of the real problem. *The reason people eat when they aren't hungry is because they are trying to tranquilize anxiety.* It is just that simple. To treat anything else is to treat the wrong thing.

Anxiety's Source

Anxiety is caused by specific imbalances in the body's energy system.

The Chinese have known about the body's energy system for thousands of years, but recently it has been more closely researched and even photographed. A Swedish radiologist named Bjorn Nordenstrom has captured electrical currents or "fields" around tissue in the lungs on X-ray film. Because they resemble the corona of the sun on the X-ray film, Nordenstrom calls these currents "corona structures." His research shows that these electrical fields exist throughout the body. Large blood vessels function as "electrically conducting cables," and bones and muscles are surrounded by their own electrical currents.

The electrical energy system is a sort of master control for the many functions of the body. As Jacques Hauton, a professor of biochemistry at the University of Marseilles explained it: "[This electrical system] is not only as complex as the circulation of blood, but it also . . . intervenes in all physiological activity." Nordenstrom himself says that artificial activation of the electrical system can have beneficial effects on disease, including improved healing of broken bones and damaged tissue. He believes that it provides a basis for the understanding of many medical mysteries, including cases where cancers are spontaneously healed, the phenomenon of oral galvanism (in which an electrical current is produced in the mouth), and the many ways in which external electromagnetic fields such as power lines and radio waves react with the body.

He says it has already been shown that a person's electromagnetic field is disturbed by strong thunderstorms and that this disturbance leads to headaches, epileptic fits, joint pains, increased traffic accidents, and other "disturbances of homeostasis" in many people.

"When these currents [in our electromagnetic fields] exceed physiologic tolerance, the organism will react," writes Nordenstrom.

He isn't the first medical researcher to find electric fields around living things. Harold Saxon Burr of Yale found electric fields around humans, other mammals, even worms and salamanders, in work he published in the 1920s. He was able to link such phenomena as regeneration (such as salamanders growing new body parts after they had been severed), tumor formation, and even hypnosis, to changes in an organism's electrical field. Burr found that these fields varied in response to light, moisture, storms (as Nordenstrom later rediscovered), and even sunspots.

Dr. Robert O. Becker, an orthopedic surgeon who has for years been conducting research into the body's electrical system, has discovered ways to use electrical fields to help knit broken or fractured bones.

And of course, one mustn't forget the electroencephalogram (EEG), that common diagnostic tool that measures brain waves. All the EEG really does is to measure the rhythmic fluctuations in voltage (or the electric waves) that occur all over the head and generate from the brain itself. These brain waves correlate with states of consciousness: Delta waves come from a person in deep sleep, theta waves come from a person in a trance, alpha waves from a person who is relaxed or meditating, and beta waves from a person who is fully conscious.

One of the ways we react to disturbances in our electrical energy system is with anxiety. My work shows that this energy system is where anxiety has its beginning. When the system goes out of balance in certain areas, we see a rise in anxiety that may lead to food addictions as well as to phobias and panic attacks. Other energy disturbances lead to depression, anger, guilt—in fact, most psychological problems.

By treating this energy system properly, anxiety can be quickly reduced.

The treatments outlined in Part II show you how to provide an external source of energy that will balance the body's energy system.

These treatments must be done near the appropriate spot on the body and with the mind tuned to the problem being treated. But done correctly, they can reduce your anxiety level (hunger) by "fixing" the energy flow of your body.

In short: When the body's electrical energy system is out of balance in a certain manner there is anxiety. When the body's electrical energy system is balanced, there is no anxiety. And when there is no anxiety, your desire to eat when you aren't hungry will disappear.

An Age-Old System

This may sound strange and new, but it really isn't. The connection between the electrical system and human health has been known for thousands of years, long before Nordenstrom, Burr, and others applied the techniques of Western medicine to its study.

The Chinese have tapped into this system for thousands of years through acupuncture and acupressure. In this ancient art, needles and/or pressure are brought to bear on "channels," points on the surface of the body that are thought to connect with the internal organs. When these channels are penetrated with a special needle or pressured, the organs are stimulated to heal through the body's response to the electrical currents generated through the channel.

These channels form major meridians that correspond to twelve major organs. There are also smaller meridians that are connected to other parts of the body.

The Chinese don't talk about the electrical fields of the body. They talk about "Qi" (pronounced *chee),* the body's vital energy. They quite literally say that illness is caused by an imbalance of this vital energy. When they seek to cure ailments, they do it by rebalancing the Qi. So in China, it isn't uncommon for colds, backaches, anxiety, or even more serious maladies like heart disease to be treated by acupuncture or acupressure.

These pathways have long been considered "theoretical," at least by the more skeptical Western doctors. Recently, however, researchers in France have photographed acupuncture pathways in the body for the first time.

Dr. Pierre de Vernejoul, director of nuclear medicine at Necker Hospital in Paris, injected a harmless radioactive substance called technetium into acupuncture pathways on a patient's arms and legs. He was then able to trace its flow along the pathways with a special camera.

When technetium was injected into the acupuncture points that have been used for thousands of years, it could be seen to move along the meridians. When it was injected randomly, however, the radioactive substance formed little blobs and didn't follow any line, thus supporting the existence of these meridians.

The researchers went even further with their work by inserting needles into the acupuncture points. The technetium moved through the channels even faster.

Researchers around the world hailed this as lending support to acupuncture's scientific validity. Now there is growing evidence of the pathways of acupuncture that has withstood the rigors of Western science.

Tapping into Unseen Energy

There are many similarities between acupuncture and the Callahan Techniques. For one thing, both techniques tap into an unseen system of energy that has a subtle but powerful effect on the human body. But the Callahan Techniques are different from the art of acupuncture. Here is how:

The Callahan Techniques Are Noninvasive

Acupuncture is an invasive treatment because it requires penetration of your skin by a needle. Acupressure is not invasive, but it can be painful, since it calls for pressure to be applied.

The Callahan Techniques are noninvasive and painless. They call for a tapping of specific areas, not intense pressure.

The Callahan Techniques Are Portable

While treatment with acupuncture or acupressure calls for needles or a table to lie on while a therapist applies pressure, the Callahan Techniques can be done anywhere. All you need is a few seconds by yourself to concentrate.

The Callahan Techniques Allow Great Precision in Diagnosis

Thanks to the diagnostic techniques I have adapted from the field of applied kinesiology, there are tests that can help you arrive at quick self-diagnosis of things like psychological reversal, minireversal, and recurring psychological reversal. These are concepts not covered in acupuncture or any other discipline, which boost treatment success.

The Callahan Techniques Are Aimed at Psychological Problems

The main difference between acupuncture and the Callahan Techniques is that my treatment is aimed at psychological problems like food addiction. Acupuncture is used mainly for physical problems like headaches, muscle injuries, or internal disorders, although there is a growing trend toward using them in treating addictions.

I approach food addiction from a psychosomatic point of

view, or, perhaps more precisely, a somatopsychological point of view. I recognize that food addiction is a psychological problem because it is ultimately the brain that is "calling out" for a tranquilizer. But it is first a physical problem because the body's electrical system—a quite physical phenomenon—has gone out of balance.

Other Advantages

There are other factors that make the Callahan Techniques a successful treatment for food addiction:

Focusing on the Problem

With most food addiction therapy, the patient is supposed to think about anything *but* food. The Callahan Techniques are different. For them to be successful, you *must* focus on food.

There are two reasons for this:

1. It is unrealistic to think that a person who is craving food can think about anything other than eating. If you want to eat when you aren't hungry, is it possible to think about anything besides eating? Not likely. It is impossible *not* to think of food when you are craving it.

2. The main reason you need to focus on the object of desire during treatment is the mind's fascinating reaction during food cravings.

When you just think about eating when you aren't hungry, the mind and body actually reproduce the act of eating to some degree. So if you just set this book aside for a moment and think about eating chocolate, you will begin to salivate. Your brain will salivate in its own way, too, producing neurochemicals that mimic those produced when you eat. As a result, your whole body reacts as though it is eating.

It is only by thinking about food that the Callahan Techniques will work in the treatment of food addiction. That is because a person who is thinking about a problem is actually engaged in that problem. He is reacting to it mentally as though it were really going on. This helps treat the desire to eat when it is happening, which is much more effective than treating it when it isn't happening.

Is treating people when they are merely thinking about a problem *really* enough? My personal experience and a substantial amount of research say it is. Here is a case study from my own practice:

An anxiety patient named Jane came to me for a peculiar phobia. She was terrified to enter a strange bathroom. At the time I was conducting research into the effects of anxiety on blood pressure, so I wrapped her arm with the blood pressure measuring device and found that her pressure was normal. Then I asked her to "think about going into a strange bathroom." Her blood pressure skyrocketed! Although she was sitting in my office, she was duplicating the experience in her own mind.

Not everyone reacts so strongly, but everyone reacts. After all, that is why the lie detector machine can work. It reads your vital signs with very delicate instruments, recording changes in blood pressure, pulse rate, skin resistance, and breathing rate. Lies cause people to feel stress, even if they are just thinking about them.

Thinking about a problem stimulates certain areas of the brain. Two researchers from Washington University in St. Louis discovered this by "looking" at the brains of subjects with an imaging device known as a PET scan while having them focus on real words and then nonalphabetical symbols. Looking at real words caused greater brain activity than looking at symbols that meant nothing. This means that directed thinking—such as focusing on a problem—is more stimulating to the brain than just doing something without focusing on the reason it is being done.

The Eye Connection

Specific eye movements are called for in some of the treatments outlined in Part II. There is no other psychological treatment that calls for specific eye positions, acupuncture included.

In the field of applied kinesiology it is well known that muscle function changes as a result of eye position. For instance, a muscle that tests strong in one test can test weak in the next if the eyes are looking in a different direction.

But why do these eye positions have an effect upon the body's electrical system? Why do they help reduce anxiety?

We don't know for sure why it is that different eye positions affect the body's electrical system, but we believe that different areas of the brain are accessed with the different eye positions. For example, we do know that the back of the brain receives greater stimulation when the eyes are open, just as the front of the brain receives relatively greater stimulation when the eyes are closed. I believe various other parts of the brain are stimulated when the eyes are in different positions. There is, however, a tremendous amount of empirical proof that these eye movements—correlated with the Callahan Techniques—make a great difference in treatment.

You will see in Part II how I use the eye positions to help eliminate the urges of food addiction.

Humming and Counting

Some of the treatments call for humming and counting. At first this might seem a bizarre way to treat food addiction, but once you have performed the treatments, you will be less bewildered by the humming and counting, since the treatment will have worked.

I use humming and counting to facilitate treating both sides of the brain. Humming, I believe, activates the right side of the brain in most people, and counting the left, thus opening the entire brain to treatment.

The way this works is theoretical since I don't have a method of observing the brain directly during this activity. But I have observed its positive effects on patients thousands of times.

Other Attempts to Explain the Callahan Techniques

People who have observed my tremendous success rate, but who are unwilling to believe that an electromagnetic imbalance actually causes the anxiety that leads to food addiction, have come up with a variety of ways to explain how the Callahan Techniques work.

When I teach the techniques to other therapists, I always tell them the theories of the group I call the "almost-believers." These are the therapists who are impressed by the astounding results but can't believe the explanation, and who, therefore, provide explanations of their own. I think it is important to present these explanations so you will know what the Callahan Techniques aren't as well as what they are.

Not a Placebo Effect . . .

The "explanation" I hear most often from the almost-believers is that the results are due to something known as the placebo effect. Sometimes a doctor comes to believe that a patient's problem is "all in his head." Since no other medication or approach is working, the doctor gives the patient a sugar pill or some other "medication" that has no physiological effect. The doctor will then tell the patient that the pill is a new "supermedicine" that will surely cure what ails him. The physician hopes that the patient will wish himself well.

For the placebo effect to work, the patient must have confidence in the doctor, the pill, or the procedure to be used. He must believe that this new approach to his problem will work.

When the average person is first exposed to the Callahan Techniques, however, he or she is often quite skeptical. Most doubt that this unfamiliar and very unusual treatment will have any effect at all.

Indeed, even after the treatment has proved successful, some people are still loath to believe it. They know they are better, but many cannot believe the treatments are responsible.

In fact, one of my early subjects was a well-known woman author who was deathly afraid of public speaking. Since I knew her and was interested in her subject, I went to hear her talk. About half an hour before she was to make her speech, I ran into her outside a hotel. She was smoking a cigarette and looking quite frightened.

"What's wrong?" I asked.

"I have to make a speech and I'm scared to death," she said.

I asked her to put her cigarette out, and then I treated her on the spot for this most common of all phobias. Afterward, she made the speech in such a relaxed manner that it was almost as if she were carrying on a conversation in her living room with close friends, rather than standing up before two hundred people seated in a ballroom.

During her speech, she stopped for a moment and looked very pleased. "You know," she said, "I have always been nervous when speaking before groups. I have avoided it like the plague. But now I am so relaxed, I think that I will make a new career of this!"

I felt proud for both of us. After the meeting, I approached her and said, "The treatment worked well." She looked at me strangely and said, "What treatment? You didn't do anything."

I had cured her of her public speaking phobia, yet she would not admit that my treatment had helped her. When good friends who knew of her fear of public speaking asked her how she overcame it, she declared that it had gone away on its own. She would not believe that the simple treatments had cured her!

I have had this happen many times, and every therapist who uses my approach reports the same phenomenon. Dr. Nathanial Branden, a well-known psychotherapist who sometimes uses my techniques in conjunction with his own work, reports his solution. He has his patients make an audiotape describing the depth of their problems just *before* beginning the Callahan Techniques. That way they can listen to the tape *after* the treatments work if they don't believe what caused the change.

There is one other reason besides denial and negative expectations that demonstrates to me the Callahan Techniques are definitely not a placebo effect. The placebo effect is chancy and can't be counted on to work. My treatments work more than nine out of ten times, which is a better success rate than can be expected for any placebo effect.

And there is one more thing. As a food addict you know

that the problem isn't all in your imagination. In fact, it's an insult to suggest that it is.

. . . *Nor Is It Hypnosis*

Some people assume that the Callahan Techniques are a form of hypnosis. Wrong again.

For one thing, hypnosis requires a series of commands to coax people into that state between sleep and wakefulness known as "hypnogogic awareness." People who have never been hypnotized usually require a sustained effort on the part of the hypnotist to enter this state.

With that in mind, note that the Callahan Techniques are done in a matter of minutes. They don't require a great deal of work on the part of the therapist or great concentration on the part of the patient.

There is another significant difference, too. The Callahan Techniques will eliminate the urge to eat about 95 percent of the time. It is easy to eliminate the addictive urge with the Callahan Techniques. Hypnosis is not nearly as effective. This difference in effective treatment rate alone is enough to distinguish between hypnosis and the Callahan Techniques.

Not "Show Biz" Either

After writing *The Five Minute Phobia Cure,* I appeared on a television show with a psychiatrist who is a nationally recognized expert on phobias. He had nice things to say about my book, but he insisted that there was no way the Callahan Techniques could successfully treat phobias. The reason he felt this way? He said that phobias are almost "untreatable" with any kind of therapy, let alone a "quick fix" approach like mine.

After he said that, I was able successfully to treat three people the psychiatrist had classified as "severe phobics." I treated them right there, in front of the doctor and the program's viewing audience. In less than five minutes a woman who was so afraid of heights she had to live in a basement was climbing a ladder; a woman who was afraid of spiders was holding a tarantula; and a woman who fainted at the thought of cats was holding a fluffy feline as her husband looked on in amazement from the audience.

What did the psychiatrist say then? He said that these phobics were cured by "show biz." Apparently he meant that by appearing in front of a television audience, they were now getting somehow magically better.

He didn't consider that it is much more difficult to treat people in front of an audience than it is to treat them in private. Besides the simple stress of appearing on television, it is harder because they are going public with their psychological problem, an added shame that patients don't have when they are treated privately. And, in any case, I achieve the same positive results when treating people in private.

Distraction Therapy

Some people think the Callahan Techniques work by distracting your attention from your craving for food.

Wrong again. For the techniques to work at all, you must *think* about food. That is obviously quite different from distraction therapy, whose purpose is to make you think about anything other than food.

Distraction therapy, by the way, has a very poor success rate. I think the reason for this is really quite obvious—try to *not* think of something you are truly craving. Try to not think of chocolate, for instance, or ice cream. Can you eliminate the thought of it from your mind? Or does it become more vivid, as it does in the minds of most people? Trying not to think of something usually intensifies it even more. Strong food addictions are quite immune from distraction.

With the Callahan Techniques, people frequently have trouble focusing obsessively on food. They may think about it, but it doesn't become the focal point of their lives as it used to.

Others have hinted that the Callahan Techniques merely delay the urge to eat. The belief here is that if control is exerted for a short period of time, it will be easier to exert greater control at a later time.

As a food addict you know the creeping anxiety that arises as you try to wait for that tranquilizing food. You know that the delay usually makes the addictive urge even greater.

When you perform the addictive urge treatments described in Part II of this book, you will see that the urge to eat when you are not hungry is gone, not just delayed, while you think of your favorite food or foods.

Effective and Powerful

Now you have read what the Callahan Techniques are not. Here is what they are: Effective and powerful tools for beating food addiction. I believe they are the most powerful tools we have to cure food and other addictions. In my own practice, I have successfully treated 80 percent of the people who have come to me with food addiction problems, showing them how to kill cravings and live happily without eating when they aren't hungry.

I have shown them what you will know from reading this book:

- Food addiction is caused by anxiety.

- This anxiety is caused by an imbalance in the body's electrical energy system.

- You eat when you aren't hungry because you desperately need a tranquilizer. Food serves that purpose.

- Food tranquilizes anxiety, but a tranquilizer does not treat anxiety. It merely masks it while causing a greater dependence upon the addictive substance and complicating your problem by creating a psychological reversal.

- Psychological reversal—a state in which you sabotage your own goals—is the reason most people fail in their attempts to stop overeating. This block against success can be fixed with the Callahan Techniques.

The most important thing you can learn from the Callahan Techniques is how to live with food. One patient summed it up nicely:

I can now sit down and have a good meal and not stuff myself. I can go to parties and ignore the junk food. I can watch TV at night and not sneak-eat like I used to. It isn't that I have to fight the urge constantly. When it comes up, I just take a moment to do the techniques and the craving is gone. I don't think about eating all the time like I used to. I just don't think about it.

FIVE

Testing Your Addiction Level

Food is one of our greatest sources of pleasure, and in the United States we have a lot of it to love.

Unfortunately, it is very easy for our love of food to become a compulsion, a craving for food when we aren't hungry. Having a compulsion about food means having an irresistible urge to eat it in greater amounts than we need.

The enjoyment of food is normal and pleasurable. But when anxiety rises, food addicts compulsively search for food to avoid that anxiety. Remember: Food can be a tranquilizer. It masks but does not eliminate anxiety. That is why you eat at night, when the tensions of the day settle on your tired shoulders and you head for the refrigerator in search of relief. Or why you eat on an airplane, when rising anxiety causes you to accept food you probably wouldn't even think of taking if you weren't trying to tranquilize yourself.

Once food starts to work as a tranquilizer (in much the same way pills like Xanax or Valium do), a food addiction becomes established. You develop the compulsive drive to eat when you aren't hungry.

A patient of mine illustrates this point very well:

Most patients who come to me to treat their fear of flying have a habit of drinking before and during the flight or of taking tranquilizing medication. Dick was unusual, however, in that he became increasingly obsessed with food before and during an airplane flight.

On the day of the flight, each consecutive meal would be larger than the last. He would start with an enormous breakfast, snack until lunch, eat a huge lunch, and then snack the rest of the day until dinner. He joked and said, "It's as though I am a convict eating my last supper."

He would pack extra food in his carry-on bag to calm his anxiety as the flight got under way. Then he would wait nervously for the stewardess to deliver the in-flight meal.

He would sometimes gain several pounds (much of that water retention) just from what he ate the day of his airplane flight.

Dick ate this way only when he had to fly. The rest of the time he ate three meals a day and rarely had any snacks. It was clearly his fear of flying that drove him to eat when he wasn't hungry.

Through the Callahan Techniques, he was able to treat his anxiety problems, not just tranquilize them with enormous amounts of food.

The solution to the problem of eating when you aren't hungry is to eliminate the anxiety. You already know that eating won't do that. It may *mask* that anxiety for a short period of time but it certainly won't eliminate it. Still, somewhere inside of you, that compulsion to eat when you aren't hungry is still lurking, waiting to rear its ugly head.

That's why it is important to know just how strong your compulsion to eat really is. The simple tests in this chapter will answer two very important questions about your addictive urges:

- How much do I really *crave* food?

- Am I psychologically reversed? Or, in other words, will I sabotage and undermine my best efforts in trying to overcome this problem; will I be blocked in trying to eradicate this problem?

Three of these tests are designed to get instant answers and one is meant to be done over a period of time so that you can establish a pattern as to when your cravings occur and determine what causes them.

These tests will give you a good idea of your baseline before starting the Callahan Techniques. But you can do them frequently to monitor your progress. You will be able to tell how much effect the techniques are having and what sort of adjustments you may need to make in your approach to food addiction.

If you want, you can think of these as a barometer, one that measures your addictive urges and shows you how far you have to go or how far you have come.

Test #1:
How Addicted Am I?

This simple multiple-choice test will show the degree to which you are addicted. Read each question and place a check next to the answer that most applies to you. *Don't contemplate the answer too much before answering.* The most truthful answer to these questions will be the one that pops into your mind first.

Answers: OFTEN = O SOMETIMES = S NEVER = N

Questions:

1. **Whenever I am with friends, I find that I steer the conversation to food by talking about favorite restaurants, favorite dishes, etc.**

   O___ S___ N___

2. **There are certain foods that I cannot resist if they are anywhere within reach.**

   O___ S___ N___

3. **I buy cookbooks and read them for entertainment.**

   O___ S___ N___

4. **I think about food when I am not hungry.**

   O___ S___ N___

5. **I refrain from flying first-class or eating in certain places because I can't resist free food.**

   O___ S___ N___

6. I have lost a considerable amount of weight but gained it back many times.

O___ S___ N___

7. Eating makes me feel better.

O___ S___ N___

8. If I am frustrated, I eat.

O___ S___ N___

9. I look forward to being alone, because then I can eat without being found out.

O___ S___ N___

10. I am okay with most foods, but sweets are my downfall.

O___ S___ N___

11. Any kind of food is my downfall.

O___ S___ N___

Give yourself two points for each O, one point for each S, and 0 points for each N.

The totals given below show the level of your addiction:

0–6 = Probably not food-addicted

7–9 = Definite food addiction

10–15 = Severe food addiction

16–22 = Very severe food addiction

Psychological Reversal Questionnaire

These three questions will help you discover your level of psychological reversal.

1. I can't seem to lose weight no matter how hard I try.

O____S____N____

2. I can't keep the weight off. When I lose anything it gradually comes back.

O____S____N____

3. I have studied and practiced the addictive urge treatments; I know that they work, but I don't do them.

O____S____N____

As with the test above, compile your score by using the following point system:

0 = 2
S = 1
N = 0

Compare your score to the numbers below to determine how psychologically reversed you are:

0 = Probably not reversed

1–3 = Psychologically reversed

4–6 = Severely psychologically reversed

Since the concept of psychological reversal is so important, Test #2 is included to provide a *physical* test for PR.

Test #2:
Am I Psychologically Reversed?

In Chapter 3 I dealt with psychological reversal, that tendency for self-sabotage that plagues almost all food addicts. Although food addicts may honestly want to lose weight, there is "something" inside of them that prevents them from controlling themselves. No matter how many times you, as a food addict, promise yourself that the overeating is going to stop, it will never happen as long as you are psychologically reversed.

When you are reversed, your motivation is turned upside down. You are geared to gain instead of lose weight.

Psychological reversal is a state that includes a number of undesirable attitudes, including: negativism, defeatism, hostility, a tendency to be supercritical, the desire to see only the down side of a situation, feelings of hopelessness and helplessness.

Some people are *massively reversed,* meaning they are reversed on almost everything in their lives. For instance, they may say they want a good relationship with their spouse, but they see to it that they have a bad relationship. They may want to get along with their fellow employees, but they don't. They may say they want to quit abusing credit cards, but their cards continue to be run up to the limit. These people are reversed; *something inside is causing them to sabotage their best efforts.*

Most people, including most food addicts, are *specifically reversed,* which means you may do most anything you want with success except stop overeating. Typical of a specifically reversed person is a schoolteacher I'll call Eva. Here is how she describes her reversal:

My greatest frustration is my weight. I can't lose any because I simply can't stop eating. I eat all the time.

My eating habits are very depressing because I can't seem to control them, whereas I can control almost everything else in my life. For instance, when I decided to become a teacher, I went back to school and got my teacher's credentials. When I decided to become the teacher of the year in my school district, I found out what it would take and went after it.

But when I decide to lose weight, I can't do a thing about it. I know that I have to eat less. But something inside of me won't let me eat less. It's like there are little people debating inside of me and the wrong side always wins!

She is describing psychological reversal to a tee! "Something" inside of her is making her eat when she is not hungry.

It is sometimes possible for a trained person to "read" psychological reversal on a person's face or in his voice. Just by talking to someone I can often identify the area in which he or she is reversed. Once you understand the concept of psychological reversal, you can actually hear and see it.

But until you become so attuned to your own body, the best way to discover if you are reversed is through the simple stretch test outlined below. This test will show you how reversal can be revealed in the flexibility of your muscles. It will help you understand why no treatment for food addiction can be successful until the psychological reversal is eliminated.

1. Warm up. Since this is a stretch test, it is important that you be limber. Stand straight, with your feet together and your knees locked. Then bend over and touch your toes or try to. *Do not bounce.*

Repeat this motion at least six times, until the hamstring muscles in the backs of your legs are as flexible as they can be. When your stretches do not increase anymore, you have reached your limit.

It is not important that you touch your toes, only that you stretch as far as you comfortably can.

2. Maximum reach. Once you are limber, repeat the stretch, this time reaching as far down your leg as you can *using only one hand.* Let your other hand just dangle at your side. Relax and keep your mind clear when going for your maximum reach. *Do not bounce.* In all of these stretches, bend slowly and reach only as far as you can without bouncing or "throwing" yourself farther.

Touch the place on your leg and keep that spot in mind. It is good to watch yourself in a mirror so you can actually see the place you are reaching. You might even mark the spot with a paper clip if you are wearing slacks. If you have an exceptionally long stretch, touch the floor with your knuckles. If your stretch is still very long, try standing on a phone book or two.

In many cases, when a person makes a statement he knows to be untrue, the stress of telling an untruth will shorten his or her stretch. Stress, in other words, can tighten or shorten the muscles, causing a reduction in range of motion.

To see whether this is true of you, try the following: Say, "My name is _____" (state your real first name) and stretch. Now say, "My name is _____" (substitute another first name, not your own) and stretch again. Remember not to bounce and keep the strain behind your knees constant each time. You may observe that you go a little farther when stating your true name than you do when stating a name that is not true. If there is a difference, let it happen; don't make it happen, but let it happen.

After using these tests on hundreds of people, I have found that the results are predictable, whether or not the person being tested knows how the test is supposed to work. Once you have mastered the test you can try this on people who don't know what to expect and see for yourself.

There are a small number of people who, no matter how hard they try, just can't see a difference in their stretches. Some of these people are reversed on self-testing, and if they do the correction for psychological reversal described in Part II, they will immediately see a marked difference. There remain a small number, however, who still do not show a difference.

If you have discerned a difference in your stretches, I will be able to show you how to test yourself for psychological reversal.

3. Psychological Reversal Test. Now stand straight, still holding your feet together. Say to yourself: "I want to lose weight." Bend over and reach with one hand. Remember the place you reached to before.

Stand straight again. Now say to yourself: "I want to gain weight." Bend over and reach with one hand. Remember the place you reached to.

If you are reversed, your reach will be longer when you say you want to gain weight than when you say you want to lose weight. This is a vivid example of the way in which a lie stresses us. Stress shortens our reach.

You can try this test with other specific areas in your life. For example try:

"I want to stop eating too much chocolate."
Followed by:
"I *don't* want to stop eating too much chocolate."
Or:
"I want to stop drinking too much alcohol."
Followed by:
"I *don't* want to stop drinking too much alcohol."
Or:
"I want to maintain my weight loss."

Followed by:

"I want to regain my lost weight."

Interpreting This Test

Are you reversed? Remember, your reach will be longer when you say you *don't* want to do something you really want to do. Reversal goes against the grain of what you really want in life. It is a devilish problem that makes you do what you really don't want to do, and prevents you from doing what you want to do.

Most food addicts are reversed, as if you didn't know that already. Most food addicts say they want to stop eating when they aren't hungry. But "something inside" is insisting that they keep eating anyway. That something is psychological reversal. It shows up in this test as the stress of an untruth that appears to make the muscles tense and, hence, shorter.

In the treatment section I'll show you how to correct psychological reversal.

Test #3:
How Stressed Am I?

The stretch test for psychological reversal is the most graphic illustration of the effects of stress in the Callahan Techniques. It not only lets you know if you are reversed, it also gives an example of what stress does to you physically. Why is this important to a person fighting food addiction? Because stress as it shows up in the muscles as restricted range of motion is one of the first signs of anxiety, which is the root cause of food addiction.

The following stretches reveal your level of stress by testing your muscles, one of the first places that stress shows itself.

This test shows how uptight you might be by testing your degree of flexibility before and after performing a treatment for stress. Be prepared to be surprised. You may be more stressed than you think.

First you will go through a series of stretches to show how flexible you are right now. After that you will undergo a treatment for rapid relaxation and then repeat the stretches. If you are stressed and responsive to this brief treatment, you will be able to stretch farther after performing the treatment.

1. Sideways stretch. Stand with your feet shoulder width apart and put your hands straight out, at 90-degree angles to your body. Now turn your head to the right and sight along your right arm as though you were aiming a gun. Turn your body as far *left* as it will go, noticing the spot on the wall where your right arm stops. Remember that spot. Now sight down your left arm and repeat the same movement, turning as far *right* as you can. Remember the spot on the wall where your left arm pointed.

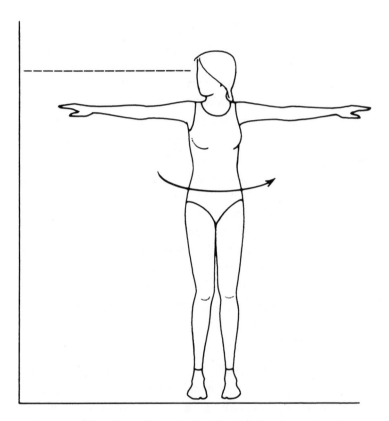

Don't swing your body. The force of the swing will give you a longer extension and a false measure of flexibility. Turn slowly, as far as you can.

Do these stretches at least three times on each side to warm up your muscles to reach their maximum stretching distance. Most people will increase their stretch response after stretching a few times and then there will be no further increase.

Eye roll (treatment for rapid relaxation). Without moving your feet, repeat the sideways stretch, only this time roll your eyes as you make your turn. Holding your head level, look down as far as you can toward the floor and then roll your eyes up as far as you can toward the ceiling. Do this as you are stretching.

If you are in need of relaxation and under stress, you should see a significant increase in stretch response after performing the eye rolls.

To test this hypothesis, repeat the sideways stretches *without* doing the eye rolls. If you are stressed, your stretch will reduce to its former point.

2. Toe touches. Stand with your legs together. Slowly bend over, reaching as far down as you can without bending your knees. *Don't bounce or throw your upper body downward.* Reach as far as you can several times until you have reached your maximum stretching distance.

You may be able to touch the floor with the tips of your fingers, you may be able to just reach your ankles, or you may be able to go no farther than your shins. How far you are able to reach isn't important. It is only important that you know how far you've reached.

Eye roll (treatment for rapid relaxation). Without moving your feet, hold your head level and look straight ahead. Lower your eyes down to the floor while keeping your head level. Then slowly bend over into a toe-touching stretch while you slowly look upward. By the time you have reached your maximum stretch downward, your eyes should be pointing up as far as they can go.

If you are stressed, these eye rolls should lead to a significant increase in your stretch response.

Repeat the toe touch again *without* rolling your eyes. If you are stressed, the stretch will return to its former point, shorter than the one accompanying the eye movements.

I will show you later how to maintain the relaxation you experienced with these eye rolls, but for now this stretch test demonstrates the effect of stress on your body's performance.

Interpreting This Test

This test for stress will give you an idea of how susceptible to anxiety you are before you start regular treatment with the Callahan Techniques.

It also serves as a poignant reminder of how stress affects us. In this case, you are able to see that a high level of stress or anxiety shows up as tension in your muscles that can restrict your range of motion. When the stress is treated by rolling your eyes, the stress is reduced and your muscles relax. The eye movements cause your muscles to relax to a greater degree than was possible without them.

Test #4:
Food and Anxiety Diary

Why do you eat when you are not hungry? And *when* do you eat when you are not hungry? These are two of the most important questions to be answered in your quest to control food addiction.

Few if any of my patients eat too much all day. Most eat three normal meals yet binge during periods of high anxiety that trigger their addictive urges. These periods of overeating often occur in patterns—you tend to eat when you aren't hungry at the same times every day.

Some food addicts do most of their bingeing on specific foods, mostly "feel good" foods like chocolate, ice cream, cookies, which contain high levels of fat and sugar. These foods are the most damaging since they add extra pounds to your body and artery-clogging fat and cholesterol to your blood.

I should point out here that not all food addicts eat only specific foods. Sometimes they eat almost anything that is available. Why some food addicts eat only specific foods and others eat anything is fairly clear to me. The specific eaters find that certain foods mask their anxiety. The general eaters find that *any* food masks their anxiety.

To help you examine the nature of your food addiction I have included this Food and Anxiety Diary. Its purpose is to:

- Expose the reasons you eat when you aren't hungry.

- Find a pattern to your addictive urges (if one exists).

- Discover the foods you are overeating (if you have a specific addiction) so you can begin the Callahan Techniques when your cravings for these foods begin.

The Food/Anxiety Diary is the most time-consuming test you will take before beginning to use the Callahan Techniques. It may be the most important information you have, however, since it reveals the patterns in your behavior.

There are some important things to remember before beginning your Food/Anxiety Diary:

Write down *everything* you eat. By this I mean every little chocolate candy you might pluck out of someone's candy dish at work. Everything counts. And besides, that "one" little candy you ate might *really* have been a handful, eaten to quell the anxiety caused by just being in the office environment.

Don't change what you eat. When people begin keeping food diaries, they often change their eating habits. You might start to unwrap a candy bar and suddenly decide not to eat it because you know it will show up in this Food/Anxiety Diary. *Eat what you would normally eat.* That is the rule for the week it will take to complete this diary. You don't have to show this diary to anyone. You are compiling it for your eyes only, to help you make significant changes in your eating habits.

Be honest with yourself. This diary calls for you to record the size of your portion (small, normal, large). Not only should you write down what you eat and when you eat it, but honestly assess the size of the portion as well. This will help you determine the type of treatment you should choose. For instance, if you eat very large portions in certain situations, then you would benefit by performing the treatment for gluttony in those situations.

Honestly recording your intake and any anxiety that goes with it will help define your treatment.

Record anxiety levels accurately. For the sake of your treatment, you must accurately record your anxiety levels. The best way to do this is to rate your anxiety on a scale of 1 (no anxiety) to 10 (high anxiety).

If you feel that your anxiety level is at 8 then write it down immediately. Don't feel like an 8 but write down a 6. Remember, effective treatment is facilitated only if you record exactly how you feel to the best of your ability.

The information you gather from this food diary will help you use the Callahan Techniques to their best effect. As an example, I offer the story of Jane, a patient who was gaining weight at a rapid rate and didn't know why:

Jane was sure she wasn't overeating. I asked her to describe her eating habits, which she did with one simple sentence: "Breakfast, lunch, and dinner and nothing in between."

I knew her eating problem wasn't an obvious one so I asked her to keep a Food/Anxiety Diary. What I found out was amazing. She was drinking a bottle of wine with dinner —*every single night!* Based on her diary, we were able to determine that she would come home full of anxiety from dealing with her very uptight boss. Then she would sit down to eat and before she knew it she had polished off a bottle of wine.

By keeping a Food/Anxiety Diary, she was able to anticipate her nervous habit before it happened. She knew that at a certain time of day she should perform the treatment for willpower and then follow it with the treatment for urge reduction. Her wine consumption dropped to a glass per night and she shed the weight she wanted to lose.

The Food/Anxiety Diary helped her see a pattern to her addiction.

You will be able to use it the same way Jane did.

DAY 1

Food eaten	Time of day	Portion Size (S)mall (N)ormal (L)arge	Were You Hungry? ("Y" or "N")	Anxiety Level (Scale of 1 to 10)	Reason for Anxiety (Specific person, place, or thing, etc.)

Were there times of the day when you ate when you weren't hungry?

YES _____ NO _____

If so, what times of day were they?
Time of Day: _____

Did you have high levels of anxiety when you ate when you weren't hungry?

YES _____ NO _____

What was the reason for your high anxiety? List below even if there are nonspecific reasons.

_____, _____, _____, _____,
_____, _____, _____, _____.

Did you eat specific foods during these periods of anxiety? List them below:

_____, _____, _____, _____,
_____, _____, _____, _____.

DAY 2

Food eaten	Time of day	Portion Size (S)mall (N)ormal (L)arge	Were You Hungry? ("Y" or "N")	Anxiety Level (Scale of 1 to 10)	Reason for Anxiety (Specific person, place, or thing, etc.)

Were there times of the day when you ate when you weren't hungry?

YES _____ NO _____

If so, what times of day were they?
Time of Day: _____

Did you have high levels of anxiety when you ate when you weren't hungry?

YES _____ NO _____

What was the reason for your high anxiety? List below even if there are nonspecific reasons.

_____ , _____ , _____ , _____ ,
_____ , _____ , _____ , _____ .

Did you eat specific foods during these periods of anxiety? List them below:

_____ , _____ , _____ , _____ ,
_____ , _____ , _____ , _____ .

DAY 3

Food eaten	Time of day	Portion Size (S)mall (N)ormal (L)arge	Were You Hungry? ("Y" or "N")	Anxiety Level (Scale of 1 to 10)	Reason for Anxiety (Specific person, place, or thing, etc.)

Were there times of the day when you ate when you weren't hungry?

YES _____ NO _____

If so, what times of day were they?
Time of Day: _____

Did you have high levels of anxiety when you ate when you weren't hungry?

YES _____ NO _____

What was the reason for your high anxiety? List below even if there are nonspecific reasons.

——————— , ——————— , ——————— , ——————— ,
——————— , ——————— , ——————— , ——————— .

Did you eat specific foods during these periods of anxiety? List them below:

——————— , ——————— , ——————— , ——————— ,
——————— , ——————— , ——————— , ——————— .

DAY 4

Food eaten	Time of day	Portion Size (S)mall (N)ormal (L)arge	Were You Hungry? ("Y" or "N")	Anxiety Level (Scale of 1 to 10)	Reason for Anxiety (Specific person, place, or thing, etc.)

Were there times of the day when you ate when you weren't hungry?

YES _____ NO _____

If so, what times of day were they?
Time of Day: _____

Did you have high levels of anxiety when you ate when you weren't hungry?

YES _____ NO _____

What was the reason for your high anxiety? List below even if there are nonspecific reasons.

_____ , _____ , _____ , _____ ,
_____ , _____ , _____ , _____ .

Did you eat specific foods during these periods of anxiety? List them below:

_____ , _____ , _____ , _____ ,
_____ , _____ , _____ , _____ .

DAY 5

Food eaten	Time of day	Portion Size (S)mall (N)ormal (L)arge	Were You Hungry? ("Y" or "N")	Anxiety Level (Scale of 1 to 10)	Reason for Anxiety (Specific person, place, or thing, etc.)

Were there times of the day when you ate when you weren't hungry?

YES _____ NO _____

If so, what times of day were they?
Time of Day: _____

Did you have high levels of anxiety when you ate when you weren't hungry?

YES _____ NO _____

What was the reason for your high anxiety? List below even if there are nonspecific reasons.

_____ , _____ , _____ , _____ ,
_____ , _____ , _____ , _____ .

Did you eat specific foods during these periods of anxiety? List them below:

_____ , _____ , _____ , _____ ,
_____ , _____ , _____ , _____ .

DAY 6

Food eaten	Time of day	Portion Size (S)mall (N)ormal (L)arge	Were You Hungry? ("Y" or "N")	Anxiety Level (Scale of 1 to 10)	Reason for Anxiety (Specific person, place, or thing, etc.)

Were there times of the day when you ate when you weren't hungry?

YES _____ NO _____

If so, what times of day were they?
Time of Day: _____

Did you have high levels of anxiety when you ate when you weren't hungry?

YES _____ NO _____

What was the reason for your high anxiety? List below even if there are nonspecific reasons.

_____, _____, _____, _____,
_____, _____, _____, _____.

Did you eat specific foods during these periods of anxiety? List them below:

_____, _____, _____, _____,
_____, _____, _____, _____.

DAY 7

Food eaten	Time of day	Portion Size (S)mall (N)ormal (L)arge	Were You Hungry? ("Y" or "N")	Anxiety Level (Scale of 1 to 10)	Reason for Anxiety (Specific person, place, or thing, etc.)

Were there times of the day when you ate when you weren't hungry?

YES _____ NO _____

If so, what times of day were they?
Time of Day: _____

Did you have high levels of anxiety when you ate when you weren't hungry?

YES _____ NO _____

What was the reason for your high anxiety? List below even if there are nonspecific reasons.

—————, —————, —————, —————,
—————, —————, —————, —————.

Did you eat specific foods during these periods of anxiety? List them below:

—————, —————, —————, —————,
—————, —————, —————, —————.

Food/Anxiety Assessment Form

Complete the following questions by looking back over your seven days of record keeping.

Were there specific times of day that I ate when I wasn't hungry? If so, what were those times? ___, ___, ___, ___.

Did I have high levels of anxiety during those times?

YES _____ NO _____

Were there specific reasons for my high anxiety? If so, what were they?

_____   _____

_____   _____

_____   _____

_____   _____

_____   _____

Did I eat specific foods when I experienced these periods of high anxiety? If so, what were they?

_____   _____

_____   _____

_____   _____

_____   _____

_____   _____

Keep the results of this assessment form handy. You will refer back to it when performing the Callahan Techniques.

Revealing Results

These four tests are simple yet revealing. Few of my patients realize the level of their addiction. They might think they have "occasional" addictions or are "a little bit" addicted to certain foods. But Test #1 (How Addicted Am I?) makes them aware of the extent of their problem. As one patient told me: "I knew I was having trouble losing weight but I never before saw so clearly just *why* I was having trouble."

Test #2 (Am I Psychologically Reversed?) is a graphic illustration of psychological reversal, that inner block that causes you to sabotage your own best efforts. In the case of food addiction, for instance, you may say that you want to stop overeating, but in reality you don't want to stop at all. This is illustrated by your body's response during the stretch test: When you say you want to lose weight, your body can't stretch as far as when you say you want to gain weight.

Psychological reversal has been called "the great internal debate" by some of my colleagues because it is a battle of wills that goes on inside a person. On the surface you may desperately want to stop overeating, but deep inside you desperately want to keep eating.

The test is physical proof of this bizarre state. It is a sort of kinesiologic lie detector test that shows how we really feel deep inside about something like eating when we aren't hungry. In the section on treatments I'll show you how to correct your reversal so the various techniques can work. Correcting psychological reversal is the first step to curing any psychological problem. Correcting reversal is so predictable a phenomenon that I have developed what I call Callahan's Law: *If a person is in a state of psychological reversal, he is unable to respond favorably to an otherwise effective treatment. If the reversal is corrected, he can then respond to an effective treatment.*

Test #3 (How Stressed Am I?) illustrates the physical symptoms of anxiety. This test also shows how quickly anxiety can come and go. Patients frequently say that until doing this test they didn't believe stress was affecting their life. Afterward, they realized it had an effect on virtually everything they did.

Test #4 (Food and Anxiety Diary) is revealing for a number of reasons. You will see patterns emerging in the way you eat. Many of you will see that a craving for certain types of food is a signal to start the Callahan Techniques. You will see that certain people, places, or situations lead to a rise in anxiety that you must mask with food.

One patient marveled at his completed Food/Anxiety Diary. "I didn't realize I was such a creature of habit until I started keeping this diary. Now I know when these habits occur and how to conquer them."

These tests are aimed at helping you understand just how food-addicted you really are. The Callahan Techniques are aimed at putting you in control of your world, making you master of your own universe.

Part II

SIX

The Callahan Techniques Treatment Guide

Now that you are familiar with my theory about food addiction, you know that:

All addictions are addictions to tranquilizers.
Whether it's food or alcohol, all addicts are attracted to an activity or substance that tranquilizes their anxiety. This tranquilizer (in your case, food) works on a temporary basis to mask anxiety. When the anxiety level rises again, so does the drive to eat. This attempt to tranquilize anxiety is why you eat when you aren't hungry.

Anxiety is caused by an imbalance in the body's electrical system. The electrical (or energy)
system we refer to is known to all who are engaged in

acupuncture as well as to a small but growing number of Western-trained scientists. Dr. Bjorn Nordenstrom of the Karolinska Institute in Sweden has conducted research on this little-known energy system, using scientific methods to examine its importance. Dr. Robert O. Becker, an orthopedic surgeon, has also conducted research that examines the body's electrical system.

Through their work as well as my own, I have concluded that when this energy system gets "out of whack," it causes a rise in anxiety. It is this anxiety that you as a food addict are trying to quell. By treating this anxiety at its source with the Callahan Techniques, you will no longer have a need to use food as a tranquilizer. You will be able to eat when you *are* hungry, without eating to quell your anxiety.

Addictions are difficult to treat because the people who treat them don't deal with the anxiety itself. Rather, "addiction specialists" often replace one tranquilizer with another. Heroin addicts, for instance, are given the drug methadone to tranquilize their cravings for heroin. This simply replaces their old addiction with a new one. Or, as Thomas Szasz, M.D., expressed it in the book *The Untamed Tongue:* "Treating addiction to heroin with methadone is like treating addiction to scotch with bourbon."

Food addicts are often told simply to eat less fattening foods. They still eat when they aren't hungry, they just eat different things.

Addictions are the most difficult of all psychological problems to conquer. But with a battle plan that attacks your food addiction from all sides, you will be able to control and eventually cure the problem.

By using the Callahan Techniques you will immediately have a sense of control that no other program gives you. By using the easy-to-follow techniques in this section, you will learn how to treat anxieties, the root of all addictions. For the first time, you will be addressing the cause of your addiction instead of covering it up.

Where other programs promise change down the road, my techniques offer a rapid treatment for food addictions. Weight loss, of course, takes time and should be achieved gradually. But within minutes you will realize that you are on the right path as your desire to eat is greatly reduced or disappears altogether.

My program to eliminate food addiction revolves around six treatments. These treatments are corrective for most situations in which you might find yourself.

Urge-Reduction Treatment

When you experience the urge to eat when you are not hungry, these are the treatments to follow. They get rid of those addictive urges by quelling the anxiety that causes them.

I recommend performing the urge-reduction treatments when you are feeling the urge to overeat as well as before meals. The reason for this is that they reduce premeal anxiety that might cause you to overeat.

The urge-reduction techniques take about one minute to perform. They are usually all you will need to eliminate the anxiety that makes you need to use food as a tranquilizer.

Psychological Reversal Treatment

Sometimes you won't respond to the urge-reduction techniques even though you have tried them several times. In that case you are probably experiencing a psychological reversal, that blocking of treatment by the body.

If you have done the urge-reduction treatments and still have addictive urges, perform the psychological reversal treatment. It will take less than a minute. Its purpose is to remove the block to effective treatment.

Rapidly Recurring Reversal Treatment

If you still don't respond to treatment, the psychological reversal treatment hasn't been effective. This happens sometimes, in which case anxiety can be reduced by following the rapidly recurring reversal treatment. The time it takes to do this treatment is less than fifteen seconds. It will almost always eliminate rapidly recurring reversal.

Minireversal Treatment

If the addictive urge diminished but didn't disappear completely, you probably have developed a minireversal. This is a psychological block that kicks in during a treatment and prevents it from working fully. This means that your urge may drop from a 9 to a 5, a definite improvement, but still not as low as you might like. By following the minireversal treatment and then repeating the urge-reduction treatments, you will experience an even greater reduction in urge and a more complete elimination of your desire to eat.

Gluttony Treatment

This is an emergency treatment for gluttony, the act of stuffing yourself with food past the point of satiation. It usually occurs when you are eating something you enjoy or when you have a need to mask a tremendous amount of anxiety.

Follow this treatment when you have eaten a normal meal and still want to eat more. Coupled with the urge-reduction treatments, it will take about one minute.

Treatment for Patience

The "all or nothing" mind-set of food addicts makes them want to lose all of their weight immediately. It is fine to want fast results, but rapid weight loss has proved to be ineffective, since it is usually followed by rapid weight *gain.*

Slow weight loss means permanent weight loss. That's a rule of thumb I use with my patients, recommending a loss of about one pound per week.

For those who still insist upon fighting the battle of the bulge a little too vigorously, I recommend the treatments to help them increase patience.

Visualization

"Nothing tastes as good as thin looks," is a motivational saying one of my patients has taped to her refrigerator. This is especially true for the overweight food addict who can visualize himself looking thin when the urge to overeat rears its ugly head. Afterall, seeing *is* believing for many people.

The treatment for visualization allows the food addict to use his mind's eye to "see" what he will look like when the weight is gone. This image functions as a source of motivation to help him reach his goal.

Prevention Treatments

As with any form of prevention, my treatments are aimed at stopping the cycle of food addiction before it begins. That usually means performing the Callahan Techniques for prevention before attending events like cocktail parties or other social gatherings in which you are likely to overeat.

The preventive treatments help you eliminate anxiety and minimize the addiction.

The Thirty-Day Food Addiction Program

This series of treatments is done every morning. Not only will they help you grow accustomed to using the Callahan Techniques, they will allow you to discover what it is like to start the day without anxiety.

The techniques in this thirty-day program take about five minutes to complete. I recommend the program for people who would like a disciplined approach to the treatment of their food addiction.

As you can see, the Callahan Techniques attack food addiction from every possible angle: before eating, at the start of addictive urges, when you can't keep the anxiety down, and even when that need to eat turns into gluttony.

Because there are so many approaches to your food addiction, it would be wise to mark the beginning of this chapter so that you can find it quickly when you want to scan for the type of treatment you need.

Also, keep in mind that food addictions are tough to treat. But they are treatable. By following the Callahan Techniques you can expect immediate control over the anxiety that causes your food addiction. And it won't take more than about fifteen minutes of your time per day!

Note: Although the treatments are repeated for different problems, what is different is the mental focus while the treatments are being done. What you are thinking about when you do the treatments is the key element for the various treatments. The thought designates the target area for the treatments.

SEVEN

Treatment for
Urge Reduction

You now know that anxiety is why you eat when you are not hungry. It creates an unpleasant state that you experience as an urge to eat. The food or "treat" that you eat doesn't eliminate anxiety, it merely masks it in the same way a tranquilizer does. As soon as the effect of the tranquilizer wears off, the urge to have another returns.

The urge for something to tranquilize anxiety is what makes you eat when you are not hungry. When anxiety becomes intolerable, the *urge* to eat becomes the *act* of eating. If you just *feel* hungry when you are not, you know it is time to use the techniques.

When you know the following steps by heart, it will take

you approximately thirty seconds to eliminate your food addiction desire. Just follow the steps:

1. Think of the object of your desire. Concentrate on the food you want to eat. If it's chocolate, think about unwrapping your favorite candy bar and then putting a piece of it in your mouth. Imagine the way it feels on your tongue and melts in your mouth. Even try to imagine swallowing it. Do this no matter what the food is, as long as it is the food you are craving.

Then, when your craving is at its highest, quantify the degree of your urge with a number from 1 to 10. A 10 indicates that the urge is so strong that you have to have that food right now. 1 means that you don't have any urge at all.

You might even want to put a check next to your anxiety level on a scale like the one below:

1____2____3____4____5____6____7____8____9____10____

Have you rated your urge? If so, then it's time for the eye taps in step 2.

2. Eye taps. With your desire for this food firmly in your mind, take two fingers of each hand and place them about two inches beneath each eyeball, just below the bony sockets of the eye.

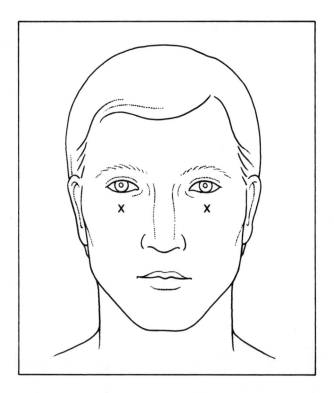

Tap those spots fifteen to twenty times, gently but firmly, while you think as hard as you can about the urge.

The desire for that particular food should drop radically, right away. Rate your urge for the food on the 1 to 10 scale. Remember, 10 is the strongest urge.

Has your urge dropped noticeably? Do you no longer have a need to eat the object of your desire? If so, go on to treatments #3 and #4. These treatments will result in your urge dropping even further. If you don't notice any change, go on to the reversal treatment #5.

3. Gamut spot treatments. Find the gamut spot. It is on the back of the hand, behind and between the knuckles of the little finger and the ring finger.

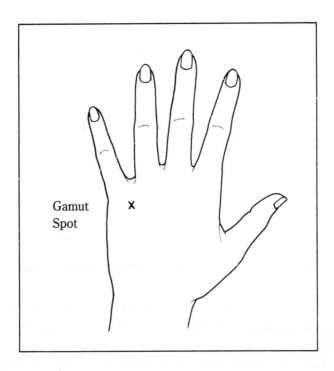

Gamut
Spot   X

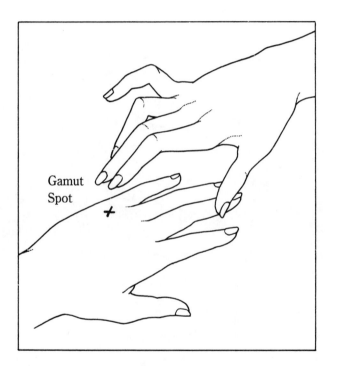

With two fingers of your other hand, start tapping that spot strongly while thinking how good the food would taste if you had it right now.

Keep tapping and thinking of the food while you hold your eyes open.

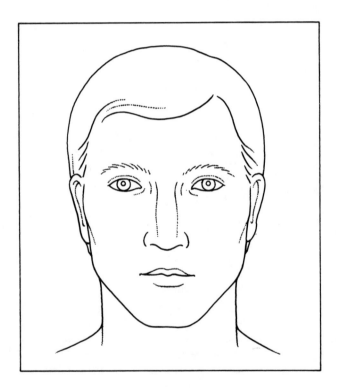

Keep tapping and close your eyes, still thinking of how good that food would taste.

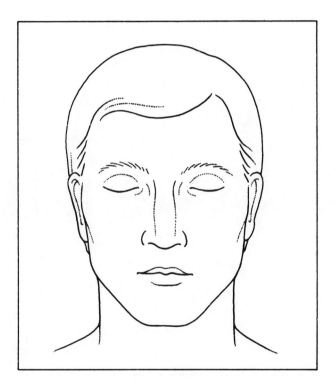

Keep tapping and thinking of that good food and open your eyes. Hold your head still but point your eyes down as far as you can and glance slightly left.

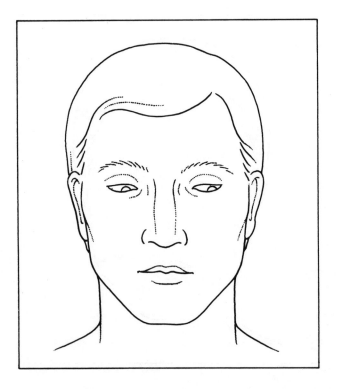

Keep tapping and thinking of that scrumptious food and look down and to the right.

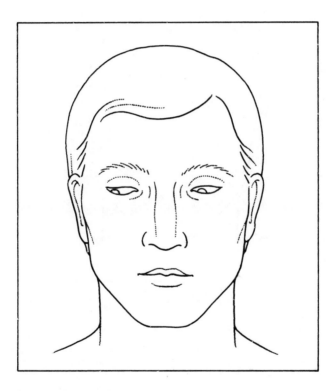

Still tapping and lusting for food, whirl your eyes in a complete circle, either way will do.

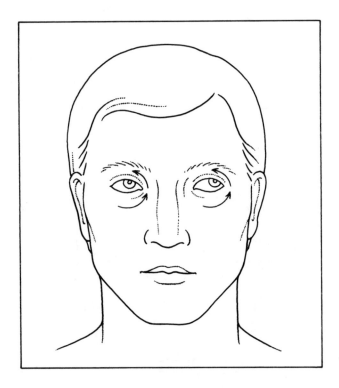

Tapping the gamut spot and lusting for food, whirl your eyes in a circle in the opposite direction.

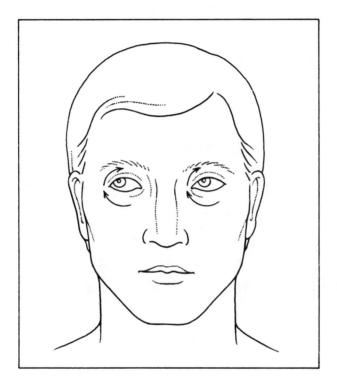

Continue tapping and hungering and hum any tune you want.

Keep tapping and thinking while you count out loud to ten.

Go back to the humming while you keep tapping and thinking of the food.

4. Eye tap treatments. Now repeat the eye tap treatments by tapping under your eyes with two fingers from each hand. Tap solidly, but not so hard that you cause pain. Be sure to think of the food while you tap fifteen to twenty times.

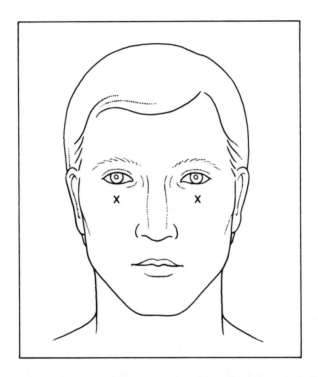

5. Tap the reversal spot. If your desire does not go down at all, find the reversal spot on your hand. It is on the outside edge of your hand, halfway between the wrist and the base of the little finger. It is the spot you would use to strike a karate blow with the side of your hand.

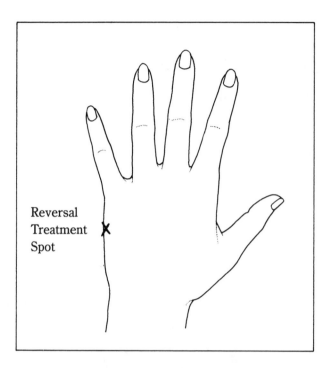

Reversal
Treatment ✗
Spot

With two fingers from your free hand, tap the center of the outer edge of the hand (either hand is okay) while you say to yourself, "I deeply accept myself even though I have this strong urge." This takes just a few seconds.

Then repeat steps 2 through 4. Remember to think hard about the food you are craving.

This treatment for psychological reversal should clear the path for the urge-reduction treatments to work.

If your desire has gone down significantly but not completely (say it was a 10 before any treatments and it is a 6 now), you are the victim of a minireversal, which is a block to effective treatment. Minireversal blocks progress in mid-treatment and prevents the urge from vanishing completely. If you fit into that category, see step 6.

6. Minireversal treatment. Tap the reversal spot on the side of one of your hands with two stiffened fingers from the other hand. The reversal spot, as outlined in step 5, is between the wrist and first joint of the little finger. It is the spot you would use to deliver a karate blow with the side of your hand.

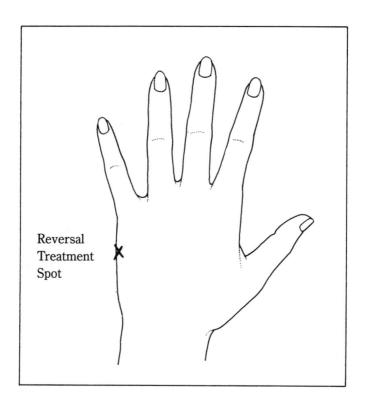

Reversal
Treatment
Spot

While tapping this spot, think about the food you are craving and say to yourself (or out loud), "I deeply accept myself even though I *still* have *some* of this problem." Be precise in your wording. Now, go on to step 7.

7. Eye tap treatments. Now tap under your eyes with two fingers from each hand. Tap firmly, but not so hard that you cause pain. Be sure to think of the food while you tap fifteen to twenty times.

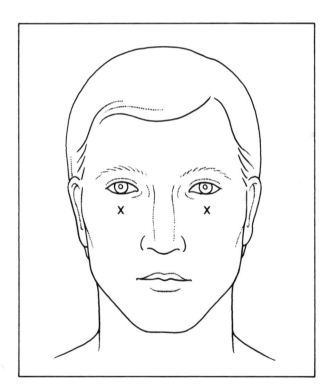

8. The gamut treatments. I call these "the gamut treatments" because the nine treatments (a gamut) are done off one spot, which I, therefore, have named the gamut spot. Find the gamut spot. It is on the back of the hand, behind and between the knuckles of the little finger and the ring finger.

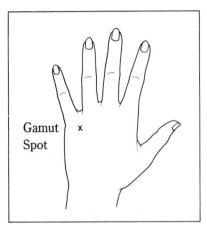

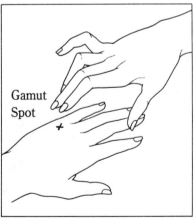

With two fingers of your other hand, start tapping that spot firmly while thinking how good the food would taste if you had it right now.

Keep tapping and thinking of the food while you hold your eyes open.

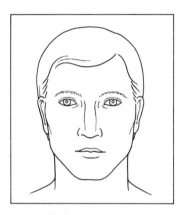

Keep tapping and close your eyes, still thinking of how good that food would taste.

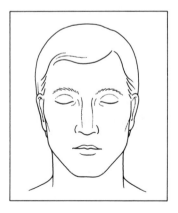

Keep tapping and thinking of that good food and open your eyes. Hold your head still but point your eyes down as far as you can and glance far to the left.

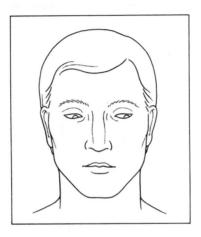

Keep tapping and thinking of that scrumptious food while you look way down and far to the right.

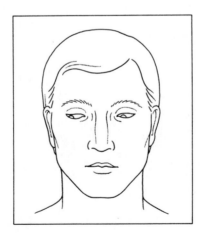

Still tapping and thinking of the food, whirl your eyes in a complete circle in either direction.

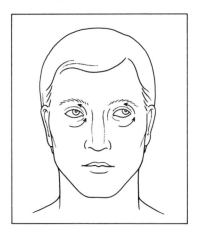

Tapping the gamut spot and lusting for food, whirl your eyes in the opposite direction.

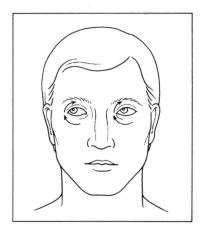

Continue tapping and hungering and hum any tune you want. "Yankee Doodle" will do, even "Satisfaction" by the Rolling Stones is all right. It is the activation of the right brain through musical thoughts that gets results.

Keep tapping and thinking while you count out loud to ten.

Go back to the humming while you keep tapping and thinking of the food.

9. Eye tap treatments. Now finish off the treatment for urge reduction by tapping under your eyes with two fingers from each hand. Tap firmly, but not so hard that you cause pain. Be sure to think of the food while you tap fifteen to twenty times.

?

I know it seems strange to think of how good the food is when what you really want to do is forget food even exists. But the Callahan Techniques are different from other approaches. Rather than distracting your attention away from the food, the techniques require that you focus on it. They are actually eliminating the source of the desire. You will find yourself forgetting about food effortlessly and naturally.

EIGHT

Treatment for Gluttony

Many people suffer from the problem of gluttony, that phenomenon of stuffing yourself with food past the point of satiation. You are already full. You are not hungry. You *know* you are not hungry. But you continue to stuff yourself anyway. Sometimes you find yourself stuffing quickly, even before you are fully aware of what is happening.

Gluttony doesn't happen with every food. It might happen when you are eating something you particularly enjoy, which also reduces your anxiety. Many of my patients become gluttonous with chocolate, for instance, or ice cream. They eat and eat because these foods bring them comfort and appear to reduce their stress.

As a food addict you probably have gluttonous tendencies. Most of my patients know from past experience when gluttony is about to rear its ugly head. Patients who need help with gluttony are usually those who say things like "I just can't resist (fill in the blank)." Certain social situations also lead to gluttony. Patients frequently report that business cocktail parties lead them to eat too much because eating is a way to "calm down" among business associates. Buffets also lead to gluttony, probably because, as one patient explained it, "When I eat at a buffet, I always want to make sure I get my money's worth."

You can treat yourself in advance for gluttony by following these treatments step by step:

1. Tap the reversal spot. Find the reversal spot. It is on the outside of either hand, between the wrist and the base of the little finger.

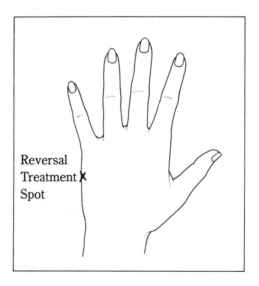

Reversal
Treatment **X**
Spot

Tap this spot ten or fifteen times with two fingers of your free hand, and say, "I accept myself even though I eat too much" three times while tapping.

2. Eye tap treatments. Now perform the eye tap treatments by tapping under your eyes with two fingers from each hand. Tap solidly, but not so hard that you cause pain. Be sure to think of the food while you tap fifteen to twenty times.

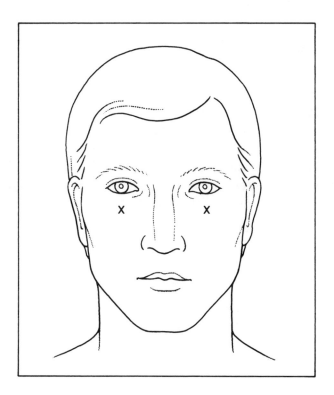

3. The gamut treatments. While still thinking about the food you are craving, find the gamut spot. It is between and behind the knuckles of your ring and little fingers.

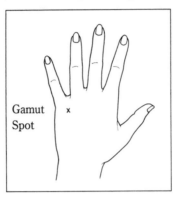

Tap this spot about fifteen times with two fingers from your free hand while you think with all your might about the foods you want to overeat. This spot is used for a number of different problems, and I have found that it often helps the gluttony problem. Still thinking about your gluttonous desire, tap the gamut spot.

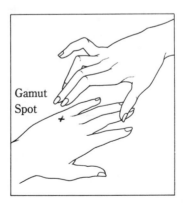

Tap firmly about ten times while you think about the food(s) you want to gorge on. Then follow the rest of the steps.

Keep tapping and thinking of the food while you hold your eyes open.

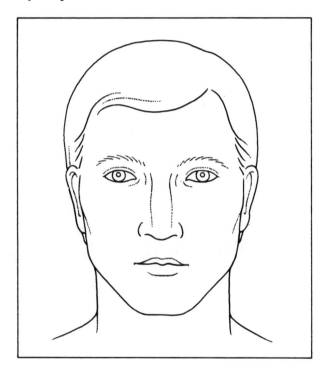

Keep tapping and close your eyes, still thinking of how strong your desire is for the food.

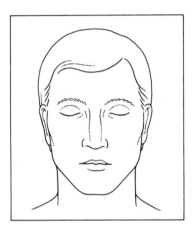

Keep tapping and thinking of the food and open your eyes. Hold your head still but point your eyes down as far as you can and glance as far as you can to the left.

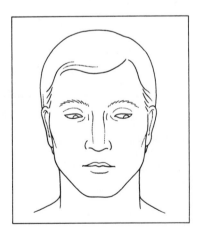

Keep tapping and thinking of the food and look down and to the right.

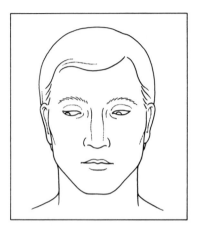

Still tapping and focusing on the food(s) you want, whirl your eyes in a complete circle in either direction.

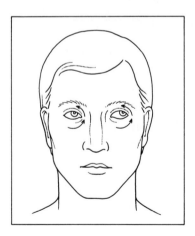

Tapping the gamut spot and concentrating on the food, whirl your eyes in the opposite direction.

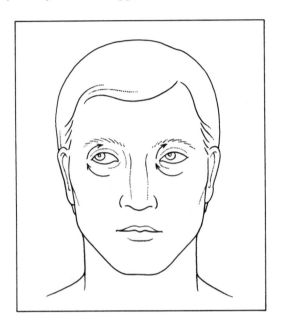

Continue tapping and focusing on the foods and hum any tune you want.

Keep tapping and thinking of food while you count out loud to ten.

Go back to the humming while you keep tapping and thinking of all that good food.

4. Tap underneath the eyes. Now finish off the treatment for gluttony by tapping under your eyes with two fingers from each hand.

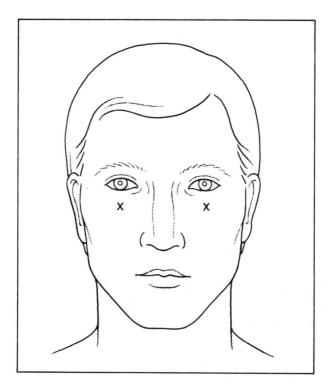

Tap firmly, but not so you cause pain. Be sure to focus on your great desire for food while you tap fifteen to twenty times.

These four steps should be all you need to overcome the gluttonous urge. Your desire to stuff yourself should be completely gone after these treatments.

NINE

Treatment for Patience

Food addicts are extremists; they want to lose weight right now. In fact, for most addicts, rapid weight loss programs are easier to stay on than sensible programs that have them losing a pound a week. The reason is that food addicts usually have an "all or nothing" mind-set. You know this to be true. Eating nothing is easier than eating just a little bit.

As a food addict you are impatient. You want things right now, including weight loss. That is why you have probably lost a lot of weight on those rapid weight loss programs only to gain it back in a matter of months. You wanted your weight loss "right now" and when you got it, you wanted your food "right now," too.

A good rule of thumb in healthy weight loss is to lose

about one pound per week. Not only is slow weight loss mentally easier, it is better for your body. Research shows that rapid weight loss causes you to lose a lot of muscle along with the fat. And when that happens, your *percentage* of body fat goes up even though your *total* body weight drops. In short, you become a thinner yet flabbier person!

That's why it's important for you to have patience and lose weight slowly instead of going overboard and losing it all too soon.

I have developed a treatment that has been helpful for some in fighting their impatience:

1. Tap underneath the eyes. With the index and middle fingers of each hand, tap underneath the bony sockets of your eyes about ten to fifteen times.

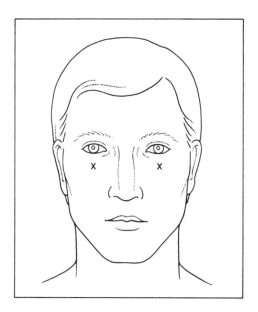

While you do this think about being impatient. I don't mean to wish you *were* patient, I mean that you should be thinking about your lack of patience, about how you would like all of your weight loss right now.

2. Tap the gamut spot. Find the gamut spot on the back of your hand, behind and between the knuckles of the little and ring fingers.

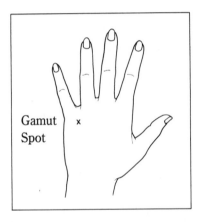

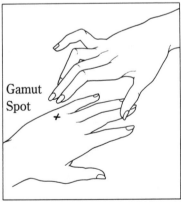

Tap that spot firmly about ten times while you think of your impatience. Then follow the rest of the steps.

Keep tapping and thinking of impatience while you hold your eyes open.

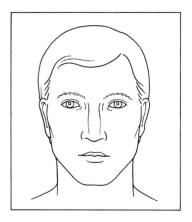

Keep tapping and close your eyes, thinking of impatience.

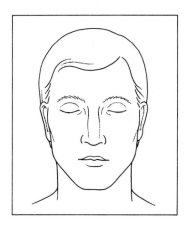

Keep tapping and thinking of your impatience and open your eyes. Hold your head still but point your eyes down as far as you can and glance as far as you can to the left.

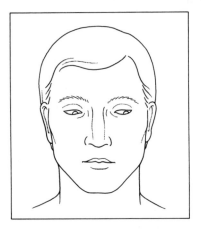

Keep tapping and thinking of impatience and look down and to the right.

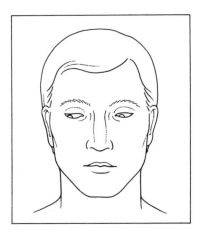

Still tapping and focusing on your impatience problem, whirl your eyes in a complete circle in either direction.

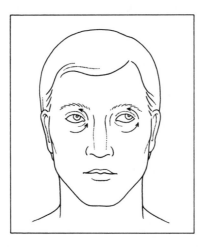

Tapping the gamut spot and concentrating on your impatience, whirl your eyes in the opposite direction.

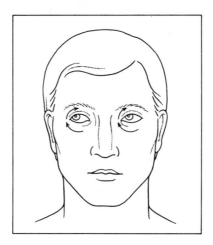

Continue tapping and focusing on your impatience and hum any tune you want.

Keep tapping and thinking of the problem while you count out loud to ten.

Go back to the humming while you keep tapping and thinking of your impatience.

3. Eye taps. Now finish off the treatment for increased patience by tapping under your eyes with two fingers from each hand.

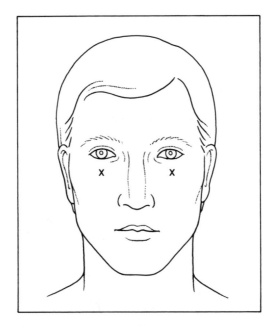

Tap firmly, but not so you cause pain. Be sure to think of your patience problem while you tap fifteen to twenty times.

This should increase your patience and help you become less extreme in your approach to weight loss. Remember, patience is your key to accepting slow, reasonable, and permanent weight loss—the kind that lasts, the valuable kind.

If your patience improves, but only slightly, on a scale of 1 to 10, you probably have a minireversal. As you recall, a reversal is a psychological block to treatment. A minireversal is when *most* of this psychological block has been removed but some still remains.

Perform the following treatment to overcome minireversal:

4. Treatment for minireversal. Find the reversal spot on your hand. It is on the outside of either hand, between the wrist and the little finger, in that area you would use to deliver a karate chop.

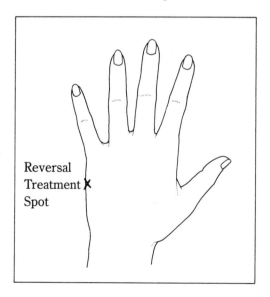

Reversal
Treatment **X**
Spot

Tap the reversal spot ten or fifteen times with two fingers from your free hand. While you tap, say, "I deeply accept myself even though I still have some of this problem."

Now repeat the first three treatments. Your patience should be greatly improved.

Since weight loss is a slow process, impatience is an understandable development. Many of my patients have benefited from these techniques for increased patience.

TEN

Visualization

For many people seeing is believing. Whether they see it in their mirror or in their mind's eye often makes no difference, which is why visualization is such a helpful tool in the treatment of food addiction.

If food addicts can visualize themselves thin and sticking to their program, they are more likely to accomplish their goal of eating less and losing weight.

Visualization comes naturally for many people. The thought of success, for example, can often conjure up very vivid images of exactly what success means. For example, people who imagine themselves being promoted to a higher position at work may see themselves driving a new car or sitting in a corner office. This conjured image is a source of motivation that actually increases a person's drive to attain his or her goal.

For a food addict, that might mean imagining how much thinner you will look in two months if you don't stuff yourself now. It gives you a body image to look forward to if you can just keep from eating now, and that mental image has the effect of relaxing you about the task of *not* eating.

Since there is clearly value in being able to visualize successful behavior, I was dismayed several years ago to find that many of my food-addicted patients found it almost impossible to visualize their success over food addiction. Most of them could visualize the most fantastic things— from flying through the air like Superman to hitting the game-winning home run in the World Series—but they could not visualize success over their psychological problem.

I think this happens because a psychological problem like food addiction carries with it an emotional investment. There is no emotional investment in flying like Superman, since that could never happen anyway. But the food addict has failed many times in his effort to stop eating, and that failure has hurt him. The emotion of that failure is preventing him from "seeing" a better self.

Can you visualize a better "you"? It is easy to find out. Simply stop whatever you are doing (especially if it is eating) and try to picture yourself as you would like to be when you are free of food addiction. For example, first try to visualize an apple. If you are able to do that, try to visualize yourself flying through the air like Superman. Now, try something harder. Visualize yourself without food addiction by envisioning yourself as thin and happy.

Can you do it? Quantify your ability to visualize on a scale of 1 to 10, where 10 represents no ability to visualize at all. If you can visualize yourself as slim, then you don't need this treatment. Just continue to think of yourself slender and without anxiety, totally free of your food addiction.

If you cannot imagine yourself free of food addiction, say you are stuck at a 6 or an 8, perform the following treatments:

1. Tap under the arm. While striving to imagine being slender, tap under the arm about ten times. This spot is even with the lower part of the chest muscle, just below your armpit.

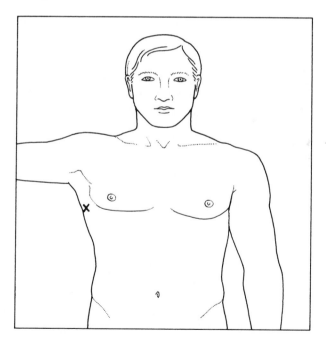

2. Gamut spot treatments. Find the gamut spot. It is on the back of the hand, behind and between the knuckles of the little finger and the ring finger.

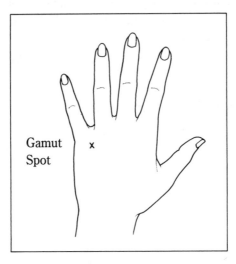

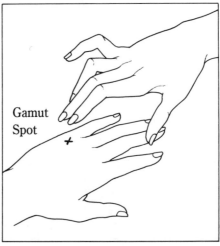

With two fingers of your other hand, start tapping that spot strongly while thinking how good the food would taste if you had it right now.

Keep tapping and thinking of the food while you hold your eyes open.

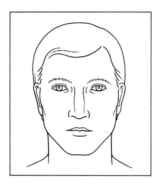

Keep tapping and close your eyes, still thinking of how good that food would taste.

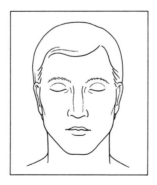

Keep tapping and thinking of that good food and open your eyes. Hold your head still but point your eyes down as far as you can and glance slightly left.

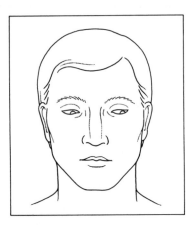

Keep tapping and thinking of that scrumptious food and look down and to the right.

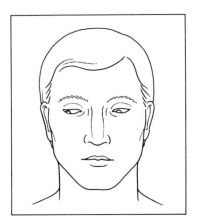

Still tapping and lusting for food, whirl your eyes in a complete circle, either way will do.

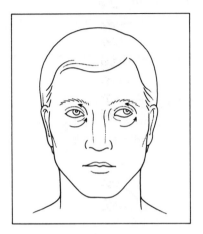

Tapping the gamut spot and lusting for food, whirl your eyes in a circle in the opposite direction.

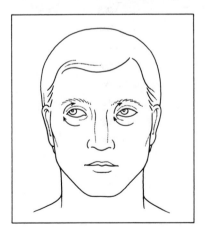

Continue tapping and hungering and hum any tune you want. "Yankee Doodle" will do, even "Satisfaction" by the Rolling Stones is all right.

Keep tapping and thinking while you count out loud to ten.

Go back to the humming while you keep tapping and thinking of the food.

3. Tap under the arm. Again, tap under the arm while striving to imagine being slender. Tap under the arm about ten times at the spot indicated in the drawing.

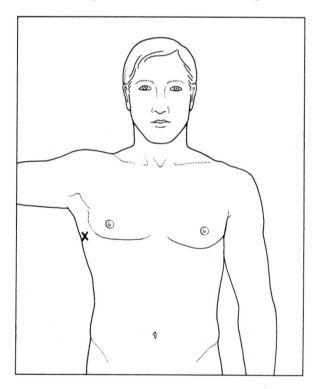

After tapping this spot you should find it somewhat easier to visualize yourself being successful. If your success in visualization has not improved at all, you probably have a psychological reversal and cannot respond to treatment at all until that block against treatment is removed. Go on to step 4.

4. Tap the reversal spot. Find the reversal spot on the outer edge of either hand. It is located between the wrist and the base of your little finger, the spot you would use to strike a karate blow.

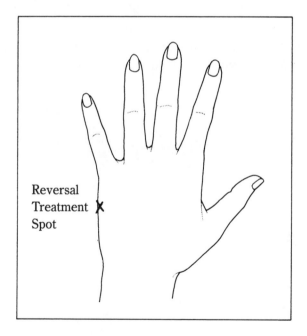

Reversal
Treatment **X**
Spot

Tap this spot with two fingers from your free hand, saying out loud (or to yourself), "I accept myself even though

I have trouble visualizing being over my problem." Do this for ten to fifteen seconds, repeating the affirmation at least three times.

This is a treatment for psychological reversal.

Now repeat step 1, which is the major treatment for improving visualization. You should notice a significant improvement in your abilities to visualize.

To make it even easier, go on to the next step.

5. Recurring psychological reversal. Find and rub the spot on the upper left portion of your chest. This spot will usually feel sore, but rub it even if it doesn't.

Please note: This spot differs from the psychological reversal spot on the hand. It is used when a more powerful treatment for reversal is needed and the simple treatment didn't help.

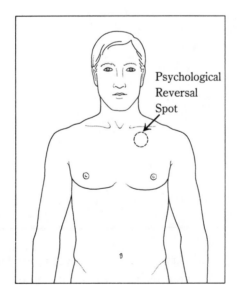

Psychological Reversal Spot

While you rub it say, "I accept myself even though I cannot visualize myself being over my problem."

Then repeat step 1, which is the major treatment for visualization. You should now experience substantial improvement in your ability to visualize.

If you responded well to the visualization treatment but are still unable to see yourself as clearly as you would like, proceed to the next treatment.

6. Minipsychological reversal. Tap the psychological reversal spot on the outer edge of the hand with two stiffly held fingers from your free hand.

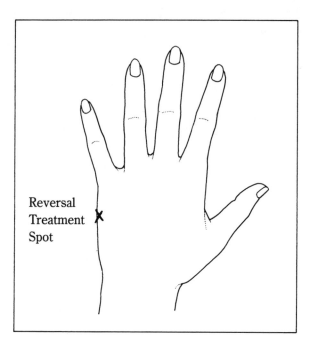

Reversal
Treatment
Spot

While tapping, say to yourself, "I accept myself even though I still have some difficulty in seeing myself being completely over my problem."

Then repeat step 1. You should now be able to visualize with the best.

The ability to "see" yourself being over a problem does not mean you are over that problem. It does mean you are able to use visualization as a therapeutic aid.

I call visualization an "aid" since it is not a treatment itself, it only makes treatment easier. After all, if you can see a thinner self in your mind's eye, you will be encouraged to overcome your problem.

ELEVEN

Treatment for Prevention of Addiction

The goal of the prevention treatments is to stop the cycle of food addiction before it begins.

As a food addict, you are often aware of a situation that might lead to overeating before it happens. An upcoming cocktail party, for instance, may be reason to perform the prevention treatments to make sure you don't overeat. Life stress that can trigger anxiety is another reason to perform the prevention treatments, since it is just such situations that can lead to uncontrollable eating.

One such example is a patient I'll call Jane. She was a "chocoholic," someone who ate copious amounts of chocolate to soothe her anxiety. Her chocolate habit had prevailed for twenty-two years, but after just a few sessions with me, she was cured of her chocolate addiction—for the time being at least.

Her cravings began again as the result of a health crisis. She called one evening and told me that X rays revealed the presence of breast cancer. The shock and trauma of the bad news had a predictable effect: She immediately began craving chocolate. She became so obsessed that she drove to the store and purchased several bars of chocolate.

That was when Jane called me. It was about ten-thirty at night when I heard her story over the telephone. She told me the bad news and then said that—strange as it might seem—she didn't want to lose control of her eating at this time of personal tragedy.

I treated her over the telephone, using the prevention treatments in this chapter. Despite her medical dilemma, Jane was able to throw the chocolate away and not lose control.

This all happened nearly two years ago. As of this writing, the surgery went well, there is no trace of the cancer, and she still has no desire for chocolate.

The following techniques are designed to stop food cravings before they start, or even shortly after. You should carry out the prevention treatments before social situations in which you are usually tempted to overeat. You should also use them when you are unexpectedly confronted with a food that you love. These treatments will stop addictive eating before it starts.

1. Eye taps. Concentrate as hard as possible on the food that you are craving. With your desire for this food firmly in your mind, take two fingers of each hand and place them about two inches beneath each eyeball, just below the bony sockets of the eye.

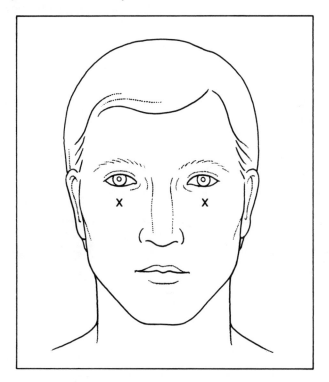

Tap these spots fifteen to twenty times, gently but firmly, while you think as hard as you can about the urge.

2. Gamut spot treatments. Find the gamut spot. It is on the back of the hand, behind and between the knuckles of the little finger and the ring finger.

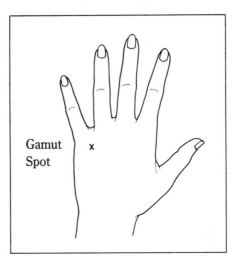

Gamut
Spot   x

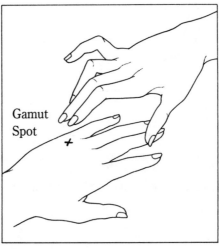

Gamut
Spot   +

With two fingers of your other hand, start tapping that spot strongly while thinking how good the food would taste if you had it right now.

Keep tapping and thinking of the food while you hold your eyes open.

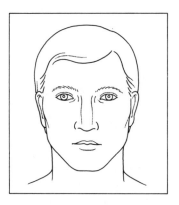

Keep tapping and close your eyes, still thinking of how good that food would taste.

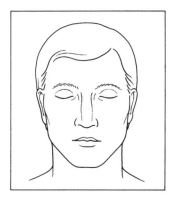

Keep tapping and thinking of that good food and open your eyes. Hold your head still but point your eyes down as far as you can and glance slightly left.

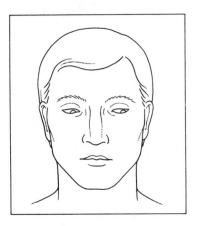

Keep tapping and thinking of that scrumptious food and look down and to the right.

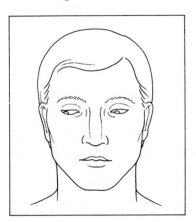

Still tapping and lusting for food, whirl your eyes in a complete circle, either way will do.

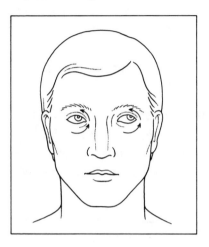

Tapping the gamut spot and lusting for food, whirl your eyes in a circle in the opposite direction.

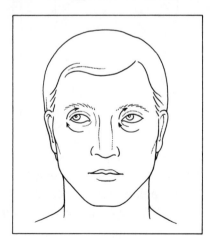

Continue tapping and hum any tune you want. "Yankee Doodle" will do, even "Satisfaction" by the Rolling Stones is all right.

Keep tapping and thinking while you count out loud to ten.

Go back to the humming while you keep tapping and thinking of the food.

3. Eye tap treatments. Now repeat the eye tap treatments by tapping under your eyes with two fingers from each hand. Tap solidly, but not so hard that you cause pain. Be sure to think of the food while you tap fifteen to twenty times.

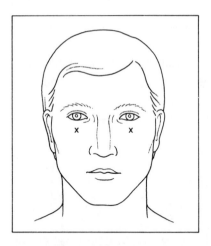

To give these treatments an extra degree of assurance, perform steps 4 through 6. These treatments will prevent psychological reversal from taking place, adding greatly to the prevention of overeating.

4. Tap the reversal spot. Find the reversal spot on the outside of your hand, below the knuckle of the little finger. It is the spot you would use to strike a blow in karate.

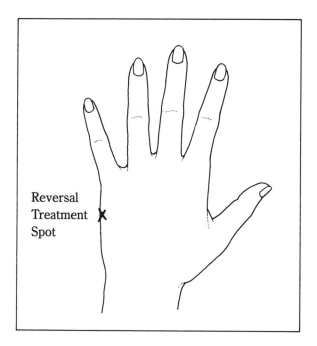

Reversal
Treatment **X**
Spot

With two fingers from your free hand, tap the center of the outer edge of the hand (either hand is okay) while you say to yourself, "I deeply accept myself even though I have this strong urge." This takes just a few seconds.

Then repeat the eye taps outlined in step 1. Remember to think hard about the food you are craving.

This treatment for psychological reversal should clear the path for the urge-reduction treatments to work.

5. The gamut treatments. Find the gamut spot. It is on the back of the hand, behind and between the knuckles of the little finger and the ring finger.

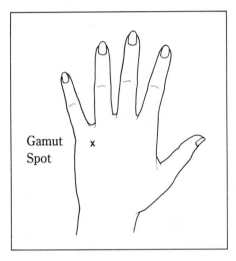

Gamut
Spot   x

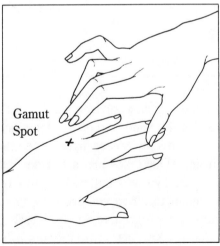

Gamut
Spot

With two fingers of your other hand, start tapping that spot firmly while thinking how good the food would taste if you had it right now.

Keep tapping and thinking of the food while you hold your eyes open.

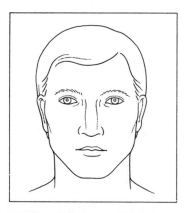

Keep tapping and close your eyes, still thinking of how good that food would taste.

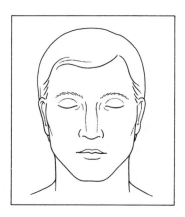

Keep tapping and thinking of that good food and open your eyes. Hold your head still but point your eyes down as far as you can and glance as far as you can to the left.

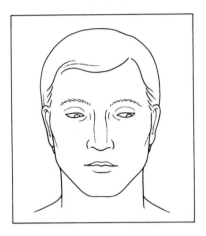

Keep tapping and thinking of that scrumptious food and look down and to the right.

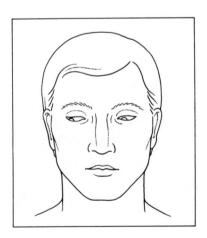

Still tapping and lusting for food, whirl your eyes in a complete circle in either direction.

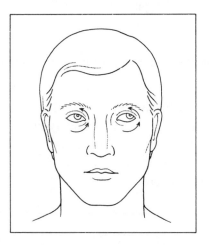

Tapping the gamut spot and lusting for food, whirl your eyes in the opposite direction.

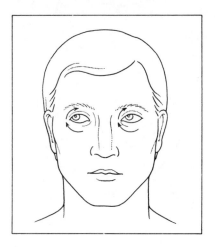

Continue tapping and hungering and hum any tune you want. "Yankee Doodle" will do; even "Satisfaction" by the Rolling Stones is all right.

Keep tapping and thinking while you count out loud to ten.

Go back to the humming while you keep tapping and thinking of the food.

6. Eye tap treatments. Now finish off the treatment for urge reduction by tapping under your eyes with two fingers from each hand. Tap firmly, but not so hard that you cause pain. Be sure to think of the food while you tap fifteen to twenty times.

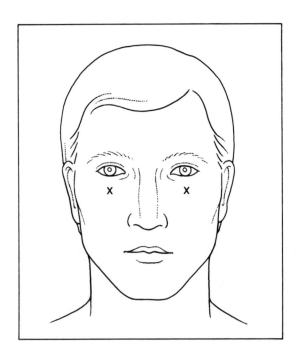

These prevention treatments will help keep you from over-eating the foods you are most addicted to, or they may keep you from eating these foods at all. Best of all, these treatments eliminate anxiety before it happens so you can enjoy yourself in a social situation without overeating.

TWELVE

The Thirty-Day Food Addiction Program

For the first time, you are treating the real cause of food addiction.

The fight against food addiction is best fought with a daily battle plan, which is why I have included a thirty-day treatment program. Following this program should take you less than seven minutes per day.

The thirty-day program for food addiction will help you become accustomed to the methods used in the Callahan Techniques. But that isn't the only reason it is important.

By following the program every day you will find that obsessive thoughts about food decrease. As the days go by you will notice that you can look at food without thinking you have to eat it.

Best of all, you will start the day free of stress, which will probably be an unfamiliar feeling. Your anxiety level should be at the low end of the scale when you finish these daily treatments, probably between 1 and 3. Record this level in the Daily Anxiety Log at the end of this chapter to help you keep track of it over a period of time. I have patients who can lower their anxiety levels by just examining the daily record they keep with their thirty-day program. They say that just looking at the way they felt on a good morning reminds them of what it is like to be without the intense anxiety that makes them crave those tranquilizing calories. It is as though reading the diary entry triggers a memory and helps them feel anxiety-free again.

Just because this is a thirty-day program doesn't mean that you have to limit yourself to only thirty days. Food addicts often go back to their addiction if there is a sudden increase in life's stress. If this happens to you, start the thirty-day treatment program again. Your recovery from stress will be far more rapid.

There are a few treatments to do before getting dressed in the morning. In fact the first of these, rubbing the recurring psychological reversal spot, is done before getting out of bed. Before beginning the treatments, mentally make note of your anxiety level. I find that some of my patients wake up with high anxiety (6 or 7) that often gets higher as the day goes on.

Do the treatments in the order they are called for and then rate your anxiety on the 10-point scale provided. There is space provided for "Before Treatment" and "After Treatment." Consider 10 the highest level of anxiety and 1 the lowest.

Treatment #1:
Psychological Reversal Spot

Before getting out of bed, lie flat on your back and find the recurring psychological reversal spot on the upper left portion of the chest. It will probably be tender.

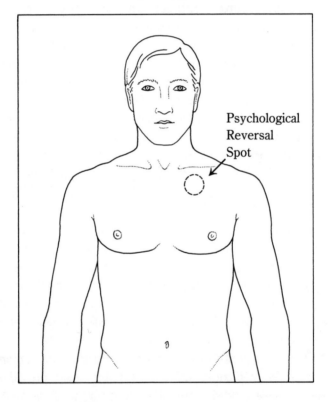

Psychological
Reversal
Spot

When seeking this spot, probe with some pressure in the area indicated. If you push hard enough anywhere on your body, it will hurt; however, you will find that this area is more sensitive than the surrounding area. Even if you don't have any tenderness, rub it in a circular fashion while saying five times, "I deeply accept myself even though I have a problem with eating." Say this out loud if possible, but if not, self-talk is okay.

Purpose

This is a treatment for recurring psychological reversal. Psychological reversal, as you will recall, is a block to effective treatment. You may honestly want to get over your need to eat when you aren't hungry, but something deep inside keeps you from doing it. It is a form of self-sabotage.

This treatment gets rid of any reversal that *might* exist first thing in the morning to keep it from interfering with the remainder of the treatments on this daily program.

Treatment #2:
Rapid Relaxation and Stretch Response

Get out of bed and check your stress level by stretching. Do this by performing two stretches and an eye roll. The purpose of the stretching is to allow you to see the difference that the eye roll treatment can make. It isn't necessary to do the stretching each time. You can do the eye roll treatment alone and it will take about five seconds.

Sideways Twist

Stand with your feet shoulder width apart and put your arms straight out to either side at shoulder level.

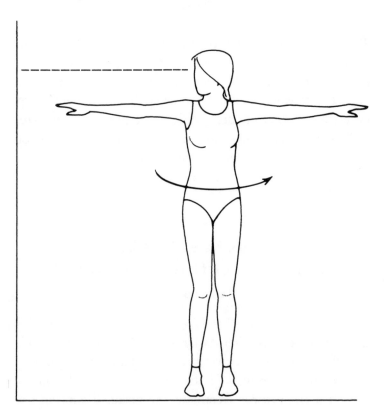

Turn your head to the right and sight down your right arm at the wall beyond. Without moving your feet, twist your body to the left as far as it will go. Notice where your right hand points to the wall and remember the spot. Repeat the same movement with the left arm. Twist to the right and note the spot on the wall that marks your maximum twist.

Toe Touch

Move your feet together and keep your legs straight. Slowly reach down for your toes, stretching as far as you can. Don't bounce! Reach slowly. The goal is to keep all variables constant so that an objective and clear measure of your stretch is possible. Repeat this several times until you are sure you have reached the limit of your stretch.

Notice how far down you reach. Some people can only reach part of the way down their legs while others can touch the tops of their shoes or even put their hands flat on the floor. Make a mental note of how far you went.

Eye Roll Stretch

This is the movement that will relax you.

Repeat the sideways twist while rolling your eyes from as low as you can look, upward as far as they can go. First twist to the right while rolling your eyes. Note the spot your finger points to on the wall. Then twist to the left, roll your eyes up and note the spot there, too. You should observe a significant increase in stretch with these eye rolls.

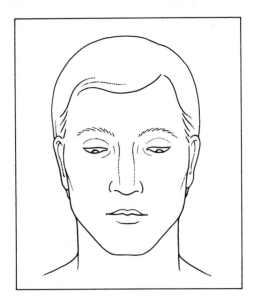

Repeat the toe touch, rolling your eyes down as far as they will go and then gradually rolling them upward, the opposite of your body movement. By the time you reach the floor your eyes will be pointed up as far as they can go. Repeat this movement a few times. Your stretch should be substantially farther than the series of toe touches done before the eye rolls.

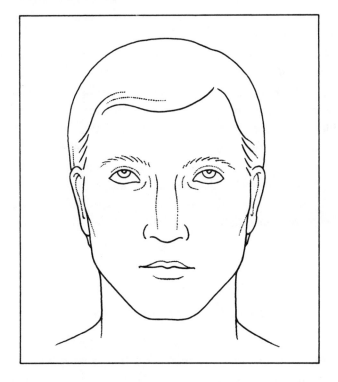

If you doubt the value of the eye rolls in decreasing anxiety, repeat the stretches again, without the eye rolls. Your stretch should return to its more limited range.

Purpose

Since relaxation is the opposite of stress, the more relaxed you are, the greater your stretch will be. The stretch response is a way of measuring your degree of relaxation. The eye rolls are a means of reducing anxiety and are a part of the thirty-day program to reduce stress. They are also in this program to demonstrate how quickly the meridians can be affected to reduce stress.

Remember: Stretching is a subjective response, as is relaxation. Some people are very flexible by nature and have long stretches. Others have tighter joints and therefore a shorter range of motion. Yoga practitioners, dancers, and athletes usually have greater flexibility than the average population because they keep themselves limber.

This treatment gives you a way of measuring your stress before and after the Callahan Techniques. But don't compare your stretch with that of anyone else. Only you know how relaxed you feel.

Treatment #3: Gamut Spot Treatment

To maintain the level of relaxation that occurs when you roll your eyes, you must now do a gamut spot treatment.

The gamut spot is located on the back of either hand, behind and between the knuckles of the little finger and the ring finger.

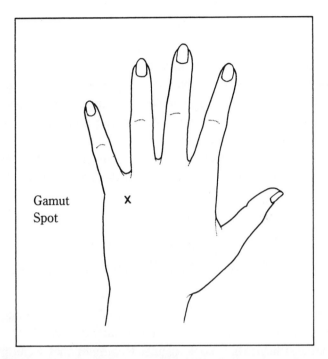

Gamut
Spot

Use the gamut spot on your nondominant hand so your dominant hand can tap energy into the spot. Make the ring and little fingers rigid and tap the gamut spot firmly for about five seconds while you slowly roll your eyes from the extreme *down* position to the extreme *up* position.

Repeat the stretches. You will see that your stretches have the same range of motion as when you did them with the eye rolls.

Purpose

Repetition of the gamut spot treatment is aimed at maintaining the reduction of stress you created by performing the three treatments. You could maintain the relaxation you achieved by doing the eye rolls—if you went around constantly doing eye rolls. But because that is both inconvenient and unattractive, I developed the gamut spot treatment to promote and maintain effortless relaxation.

Emergency Treatment: If All Else Failed . . .

If none of the above treatments resulted in a significant increase in your stretch or a lower anxiety level, then you may still have that block against treatment that I call psychological reversal. Although we tried to correct for it with treatment #1, that treatment may not have been enough. You can tell if you have a reversal by measuring your anxiety level. If it was high before treatment and is at the same level afterward, then you are probably reversed.

To treat for this problem, find the psychological reversal spot on your hand, about halfway up the outer edge at the spot you would use to deliver a karate blow.

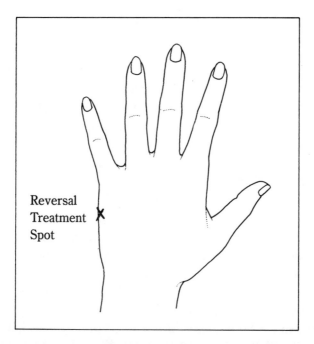

Reversal Treatment Spot

Tap that spot while saying, "I accept myself even if I don't increase my stretch." Repeat that three times while tapping the spot.

Then, tap the gamut spot and repeat the eye rolls.

Now repeat the stretches in treatment #2 without doing the eye rolls. You should observe a distinct increase in your stretch.

When these treatments are completed, enter your before and after anxiety levels in the daily diary.

Exercise

Since exercise reduces anxiety, it is an important part of my program to eliminate food addictions. This presents a dilemma for many people with food addictions, since they often have difficulty staying on an exercise program.

Still, I consider exercise an important aspect of the thirty-day program. It isn't mandatory that you exercise for the Callahan Techniques to work, but I assure you they will work better if you are on even a mild fitness routine.

I am providing one here for those of you who don't follow a regular program of exercise and might want an easy and effective one to start with. It was adapted from one developed by Professor Laurence E. Morehouse of the human performance laboratory at the University of California at Los Angeles, who is a leading expert in fitness, and presented in his book *Total Fitness in Thirty Minutes a Week* (coauthored with Leonard Gross).

I recommend this program because it is an easy way to achieve strength, flexibility, and aerobic power as well as a substantial reduction in anxiety. Morehouse recommends that you do this program three times a week for two months and then go on to more advanced workouts. It is a beginning program, for both men and women, that takes about ten minutes per session, builds gradually, and never causes you to strain.

If you aren't already on an exercise program, this is a good place to start.

Limbering (One Minute)

The object of these exercises is to warm up your muscles. Spend about fifteen seconds on each exercise:

1. Reach up as high as you can toward the ceiling with one arm. Your hand should be directly over your head. It's a prolonged reach we're after. Feel the stretch all the way to your ankle, all the way along your side. When you feel all stretched out, drop your arm and repeat the exercise with your other arm. Be a cat; stretch to the outer limit.

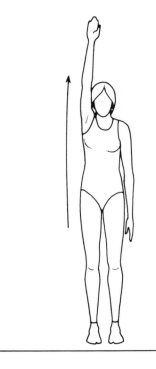

2. Arms extended sideward, twist your trunk in one direction as far as you can turn. Then twist in the opposite direction. In the military, this exercise is performed with a snap. These are nonmilitary proceedings. No snaps, please.

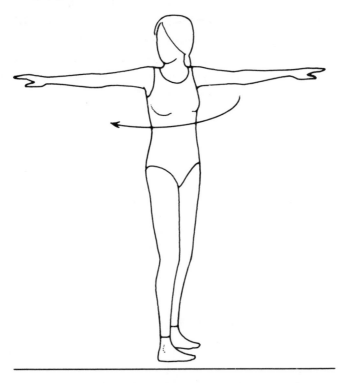

3. Lean over and hold yourself behind the knees and gently pull your shoulders toward your knees. Don't use force. Don't use momentum. Just an easy stretch. Some people will get closer to their knees than others.

It's all relative to your condition. If you're in terrible shape, even gaining near proximity to your knees is a triumph; and you've done yourself a world of good. If you're already fairly supple, you should soon get fairly close.

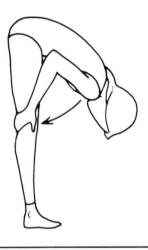

4. Turn your head to the side, with your chin over the top of your left shoulder. Place your left hand against your chin, on the right side of your face. Place your right hand on your head from behind. With both hands, now turn your head just a little farther than it can turn on its own. Gently, please. Don't try to jerk your head or snap it. Now reverse the process, with your chin over your right shoulder, your right hand against the left side of your face, the left hand grasping the head from behind. Slowly stretch your neck muscles.

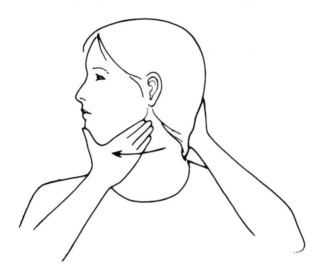

In the first few sessions, one performance of each of the movements is sufficient. Later you may wish to do them twice or even three times. But do them in a leisurely, relaxed manner.

Now that you are stretched and limbered you are ready to develop muscle tissue.

Muscle Buildup (Four Minutes)

During the next four minutes you are going to concentrate on developing muscle fiber by pumping your muscles against resistance. As you continue to exercise, it will be easier for you to overcome the same resistance. So you should gradually increase the resistance.

You'll do two exercises, alternating them for a full four

minutes. The first will expand the muscles of your shoulders, chest, and arms. The second will expand the muscles of your abdomen and back. Don't worry about your legs, they'll get all the exercise they need at the end of the session.

1. Expansion pushaways. Stand a little beyond arm's reach from a wall. Put your hands against the wall at the height of your shoulders. Lean forward until your chest comes near the wall. Then push away until you're back to the starting position. If that's too hard, step in closer. Do the exercise about fifteen or twenty times, or until the exertion begins to feel heavy. This is one set.

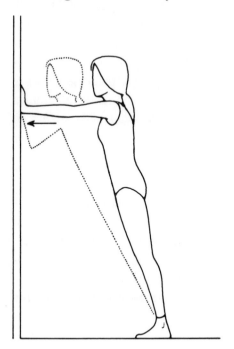

When you can do a set of twenty or more with ease, move a bit farther away from the wall to create a slight increase in difficulty.

In successive workouts you'll be able to do more repetitions. Just keep moving away from the wall until you find the position that gives a moderate effort. If you can do a set of more than twenty pushaways before the exertion begins to feel heavy, shift to a new position next time.

Some people will find from the outset that the pushaway from the wall is too easy. In that event, repeat the exercise using a kitchen counter or a bathroom sink, or a chest of drawers—anything that lowers the height of your hands below the height of your shoulders. If you can do only fifteen pushaways before the exertion becomes heavy, you've found your starting place. We want an exercise that begins to feel difficult after fifteen executions.

Eventually you will be able to begin these pushaways from lower and lower heights: the wall, a countertop, a tabletop, a chair, and finally the floor. The goal is to get you down to the floor, doing push-ups.

2. Expansion sitbacks. This exercise works the muscles of your abdominal wall.

The abdominal muscles are the hardest ones to involve in beneficial exercise. They are supportive muscles, not meant to flex isotonically, meaning with movement. They function isometrically, holding without moving, and that's the way they should be exercised.

These are not ordinary sit-ups. A sit-up calls on the hip flexor muscles to do most of the work and leaves the abdominal muscles out of it.

Expansion sitbacks work only the abdominal muscles. Sit on the floor with your feet hooked under a piece of furniture. Bend your knees. Move your chest as close to your knees as you can, then place your hands on your abdomen so you can feel the muscle action.

Move back away from your knees until you feel your abdominal muscles come into play. You can tell when this happens by probing your abdominal muscles with your fingers. Lower yourself back a few inches and then return. If that was easy, go back a few more inches and return. Keep it up until you find a spot where you are getting a mild workout.

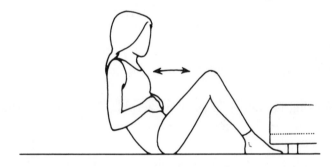

Start with a degree of effort that enables you to hold the position for fifteen to twenty seconds. During the last few seconds, the belly muscles should begin to quiver.

Work up to a full twenty-second sitback before the quivering commences, then try a deeper sitback. When your back is brushing the floor, and you can hold the sitback for twenty seconds or more, "load up" the exercise by moving your arms. Until now you've been holding them in front of you, with your hands on your stomach. Now fold them on your chest in order to increase the resistance. That little change will take you back to fifteen seconds per set; you may even need to make your sitback more shallow for a few days.

When this position has been mastered, move your hands behind your head. Finally, move your arms over your head. Caution: Don't swing your arms. They're elevated for added weight, and should not be used for momentum.

Do several sets of these sitbacks until you have done them for four minutes.

Aerobics (Five Minutes)

During this phase, you can choose any steady, easy activity that will raise your heart rate to the proper level for five minutes.

Walking is fine, as is running, aerobic dance, or just running in place. The key is to elevate your heart rate to at least 60 percent (but no more than 90 percent) of your maximum heart rate. You can figure that target heart rate with the following equation:

$220 -$ (your age) $\times$ .60 to .90 = target heart rate

For example, a forty-year old who wants to exercise at 60 percent of his or her maximum heart rate would figure it this way:

$220 - 40 = 180 \times .60 = 108$ beats per minute.

Count your heartbeats by finding the carotid artery that passes up the neck and supplies the head with blood. Place your index and middle fingers on either side of your neck right below your jawbone and count the number of heart-beats for fifteen seconds. Multiply that number times four to get beats per minute.

An easier way to gauge exercise intensity is to exercise to the point of breathlessness, but not beyond the point at which you can talk or carry on a conversation.

This daily routine combining the Callahan Techniques and exercise will decrease your anxiety level immediately. This is often all people need to gain control over their food addiction, and the combination can be done in about fifteen minutes per day!

Keep track of your daily anxiety levels in the before and after diary provided at the end of this chapter. This method of self-rating is the quickest and among the most accurate methods of telling how anxious you are. After all, no one knows better than you just how much anxiety you have. That is because no one knows better than you what makes you feel stressed or how anxious you will become after experiencing a stressor.

You should see a marked difference each day and over the course of the thirty days.

Daily Anxiety Log
(30-Day Record of the Effects on Anxiety of the Callahan Techniques)

Day 1
BEFORE TREATMENT:

1____2____3____4____5____6____7____8____9____10____

AFTER TREATMENT:

1____2____3____4____5____6____7____8____9____10____

Day 2
BEFORE TREATMENT:

1____2____3____4____5____6____7____8____9____10____

AFTER TREATMENT:

1____2____3____4____5____6____7____8____9____10____

Day 3
BEFORE TREATMENT:

1____2____3____4____5____6____7____8____9____10____

AFTER TREATMENT:

1____2____3____4____5____6____7____8____9____10____

Day 4
BEFORE TREATMENT:

1____2____3____4____5____6____7____8____9____10____

AFTER TREATMENT:

1____2____3____4____5____6____7____8____9____10____

Day 5
BEFORE TREATMENT:

1___2___3___4___5___6___7___8___9___10___

AFTER TREATMENT:

1___2___3___4___5___6___7___8___9___10___

Day 6
BEFORE TREATMENT:

1___2___3___4___5___6___7___8___9___10___

AFTER TREATMENT:

1___2___3___4___5___6___7___8___9___10___

Day 7
BEFORE TREATMENT:

1___2___3___4___5___6___7___8___9___10___

AFTER TREATMENT:

1___2___3___4___5___6___7___8___9___10___

Day 8
BEFORE TREATMENT:

1___2___3___4___5___6___7___8___9___10___

AFTER TREATMENT:

1___2___3___4___5___6___7___8___9___10___

Day 9
BEFORE TREATMENT:

1____2____3____4____5____6____7____8____9____10____

AFTER TREATMENT:

1____2____3____4____5____6____7____8____9____10____

Day 10
BEFORE TREATMENT:

1____2____3____4____5____6____7____8____9____10____

AFTER TREATMENT:

1____2____3____4____5____6____7____8____9____10____

Day 11
BEFORE TREATMENT:

1____2____3____4____5____6____7____8____9____10____

AFTER TREATMENT:

1____2____3____4____5____6____7____8____9____10____

Day 12
BEFORE TREATMENT:

1____2____3____4____5____6____7____8____9____10____

AFTER TREATMENT:

1____2____3____4____5____6____7____8____9____10____

Day 13
BEFORE TREATMENT:

1____2____3____4____5____6____7____8____9____10____

AFTER TREATMENT:

1____2____3____4____5____6____7____8____9____10____

Day 14
BEFORE TREATMENT:

1____2____3____4____5____6____7____8____9____10____

AFTER TREATMENT:

1____2____3____4____5____6____7____8____9____10____

Day 15
BEFORE TREATMENT:

1____2____3____4____5____6____7____8____9____10____

AFTER TREATMENT:

1____2____3____4____5____6____7____8____9____10____

Day 16
BEFORE TREATMENT:

1____2____3____4____5____6____7____8____9____10____

AFTER TREATMENT:

1____2____3____4____5____6____7____8____9____10____

Day 17
BEFORE TREATMENT:

1____2____3____4____5____6____7____8____9____10____

AFTER TREATMENT:

1____2____3____4____5____6____7____8____9____10____

Day 18
BEFORE TREATMENT:

1____2____3____4____5____6____7____8____9____10____

AFTER TREATMENT:

1____2____3____4____5____6____7____8____9____10____

Day 19
BEFORE TREATMENT:

1____2____3____4____5____6____7____8____9____10____

AFTER TREATMENT:

1____2____3____4____5____6____7____8____9____10____

Day 20
BEFORE TREATMENT:

1____2____3____4____5____6____7____8____9____10____

AFTER TREATMENT:

1____2____3____4____5____6____7____8____9____10____

Day 21
BEFORE TREATMENT:

1___2___3___4___5___6___7___8___9___10___

AFTER TREATMENT:

1___2___3___4___5___6___7___8___9___10___

Day 22
BEFORE TREATMENT:

1___2___3___4___5___6___7___8___9___10___

AFTER TREATMENT:

1___2___3___4___5___6___7___8___9___10___

Day 23
BEFORE TREATMENT:

1___2___3___4___5___6___7___8___9___10___

AFTER TREATMENT:

1___2___3___4___5___6___7___8___9___10___

Day 24
BEFORE TREATMENT:

1___2___3___4___5___6___7___8___9___10___

AFTER TREATMENT:

1___2___3___4___5___6___7___8___9___10___

Day 25
BEFORE TREATMENT:

1____2____3____4____5____6____7____8____9____10____

AFTER TREATMENT:

1____2____3____4____5____6____7____8____9____10____

Day 26
BEFORE TREATMENT:

1____2____3____4____5____6____7____8____9____10____

AFTER TREATMENT:

1____2____3____4____5____6____7____8____9____10____

Day 27
BEFORE TREATMENT:

1____2____3____4____5____6____7____8____9____10____

AFTER TREATMENT:

1____2____3____4____5____6____7____8____9____10____

Day 28
BEFORE TREATMENT:

1____2____3____4____5____6____7____8____9____10____

AFTER TREATMENT:

1____2____3____4____5____6____7____8____9____10____

Day 29
BEFORE TREATMENT:

1____2____3____4____5____6____7____8____9____10____

AFTER TREATMENT:

1____2____3____4____5____6____7____8____9____10____

Day 30
BEFORE TREATMENT:

1____2____3____4____5____6____7____8____9____10____

AFTER TREATMENT:

1____2____3____4____5____6____7____8____9____10____

AFTERWORD

As you know, the Callahan Techniques are not a diet. They are extremely effective treatments for food addiction. But they are not a diet.

There are plenty of diet programs on the market, some very good, and some not so good. In fact, diet programs are as changeable as the weather, with a new one coming along almost every day. These new diets keep coming out because, frankly, the old ones don't work for long-term weight loss. Despite the fact that, according to the *New York Times,* $30 billion is spent each year on weight loss (which is one reason it is called the weight loss industry) only 3 percent of the people who lose weight are able to keep it off for more than two years.

The reason these people can't keep the weight off is because they are food-addicted. They can win the food fight for a while, but as food addicts they will eventually be forced to use food as a tranquilizer. Eating is the only way they know of calming down.

But now that you know the facts about food addiction you can control it and treat it with the Callahan Techniques. These treat the underlying cause of food addiction—the anxiety—and replace it with a deep feeling of effortless relaxation and confidence.

The Callahan Techniques are truly in the vanguard of addiction treatment. So you should be congratulated for being ahead of your time. With the Callahan Techniques you are treating the cause of addiction, not just the symptoms. When people see you tapping under your eyes and ask what you are doing, you can tell them just that. If they are food-addicted, in time you will probably see them tapping, too.

GLOSSARY

Addiction: A psychological dependency upon some substance or activity that causes some degree of harm to the person and is very difficult to eradicate. Addictions are to be distinguished from habits, which are relatively easy to eradicate. Most addicts also suffer from psychological reversal (see below). The addict usually knows that he should stop indulging his addiction but is unable to do so.

Addictive Urge: The strength of the desire or need an addict experiences to indulge or engage in his addiction at any particular moment. An addictive urge can be expressed in degrees from 1 to 10 where 10 represents an urge that is irresistible and 1 is the complete absence of desire or interest.

Anxiety: A type of fear that is pervasive, unfocused, and extremely unpleasant. It is my belief that tranquilizing or masking anxiety creates addiction. In other words, no anxiety no addiction.

Applied Kinesiology: An innovative method of diagnosis and treatment developed by Dr. George Goodheart that involves the standardized testing of muscles in order to ascertain the causes of various problems.

Anorexia: A severe phobia involving an unreasonable fear of eating and gaining weight, and a distortion of body image that causes the patient to believe she is overweight, even though she "knows" she is not. Can be life-threatening.

Bulimia: A food addiction problem in which the patient indulges in binge eating and attempts to keep weight under control by self-purging to expel food.

Cure: The eradication of a problem. When a person no longer gives a problem any consideration and attains freedom of action and thought, we consider him cured. In order to be pronounced, a cure must last a reasonable amount of time. We have found that with most problems, our cures last (at present) for at least ten years (that's when our first treatments were done). Addiction is the hardest problem to cure because extreme stress can send some significantly helped addicts back to their favorite tranquilizer.

Energy System: A palpable, tangible series of electric or electromagnetic circuits or meridians throughout the body that appear to act as a governing force in healing. Problems are created when this system is not in balance.

Gamut Spot: A treatment spot located on the back of the hand, behind and between the knuckles of the little and the ring fingers. It is the treatment spot for the series of treatments known as the gamut treatment.

Gamut Treatment: A series of nine treatments done while tapping the gamut spot on the back of the hand. This series of treatments, which is convenient to see as a unit, is done for most problems and is inserted between repetitions of a particular treatment for the problem. For example, for the addictive urge treatment, you tap under your eyes and then follow with the gamut series and then repeat the tapping under the eyes. If there is no psychological reversal present the addictive urge should be completely gone.

Massive Psychological Reversal: A condition of psychological reversal (see below) in most of the major areas of a person's life.

Meridian: A concept from the field of acupuncture that refers to specific pathways or channels of body energy.

Minireversal: (See Psychological Reversal below.) A condition of psychological reversal that takes place *during* an effective treatment and prevents the treatment from completely eradicating a problem. Fixing the minireversal and repeating the treatment will usually result in the complete eradication of the problem.

Phobia: A persistent, irrational fear directed toward some object or situation. The victim usually knows that his fear makes no sense but this knowledge does not help him to overcome it.

Physiological Addiction: Physical dependence on some substance such as heroin or nicotine. I believe that physiological dependency upon a drug or substance has been overemphasized and has taken the focus off the major problem, which is psychological. For example, there is evidence that addiction to nicotine is physical, but the physical addiction is trivial compared to the psychological addiction.

Psychological Reversal: A state or condition that prevents natural healing and blocks otherwise effective treatments from working. Usually accompanied by negative attitudes and self-sabotage that leads to self-defeating behavior. I suspect a psychological reversal when one of my otherwise effective treatments does not work. The presence of psychological reversal is confirmed when the treatment for reversal is done and the very treatment that did not work a moment before now works. Psychological reversal is usually confined to particular areas of one's life but may occur in any area, such as personal relationships, athletics, social life, education, love, sex, or health. Chronic problems usually have an element of psychological reversal. Psychological reversal is almost always present in addiction problems.

Psychological Reversal Treatment Spot: A spot located halfway between the base of the little finger and the wrist, on the outer edge of the hand. Treatment here usually proves to be adequate for most reversal problems.

Recurring Psychological Reversal Treatment Area: An area on the upper left chest that is sometimes tender or sore. Rubbing this area has proved to be an effective treatment for psychological reversal that keeps recurring.

Self-Acceptance: Acknowledging one's shortcomings without denigrating oneself for having them. Self-acceptance is a powerful aid in helping to promote change. The essence of self-acceptance is expressed by Lewis Thomas's description of Montaigne *(A Long Line of Cells,* p. 206) ". . . he likes himself, to be sure, but is never swept off his feet after the fashion of bores. He is fond of his mind, and affectionately entertained by everything in his head."

Self-Sabotage: A condition in which the person is his own worst enemy. He engages in behavior that goes against his self-interest and in extreme form is self-destructive. We find this condition associated with the state of psychological reversal.

Tranquilizer: A substance or activity that temporarily and partially masks, but does not actually help, anxiety. The tranquilizing of anxiety, I believe, is what leads to addiction problems.

Withdrawal: The suffering an addict undergoes when he cannot indulge in his favorite tranquilizer (substance or behavioral). Withdrawal, in my opinion, is actually an anxiety attack. Appropriate treatment for anxiety (not tranquilizers) will usually result in an immediate reduction in withdrawal that will last for varying periods and will need to be repeated.

REFERENCES

1. Becker, Robert O., and Selden, Gary. *The Body Electric.* New York: Morrow, 1985.

2. Blaich, Robert. "Applied Kinesiology and Human Performance." *Selected Papers of the International College of Applied Kinesiology,* pp. 7–15. 1988.

3. Callahan, Roger. "Psychological Reversal." *Selected Papers of the International College of Applied Kinesiology,* pp. 79–96. Winter, 1981.

4. Callahan, Roger, with Levine, Karen. *It Can Happen to You.* New York: New American Library, 1983.

5. Callahan, Roger. *Five Minute Phobia Cure.* Wilmington, Del.: Enterprise, 1985.

6. Callahan, Roger. "Successful Psychotherapy by Radio and Telephone." International College of Applied Kinesiology. Winter, 1987.

7. Melzack, Ronald. "The Tragedy of Needless Pain." *Scientific American,* Vol. 262, No. 2, Feb., 1990.

8. Morehouse, L., and Gross, L. *Total Fitness in 30 Minutes a Week.* New York: Simon & Schuster, 1975.

9. Nordenstrom, Bjorn. *Biologically Closed Electric Circuits: Clinical, Experimental, and Theoretical Evidence for an Additional Circulatory System.* Stockholm: Nordic, 1983.

10. Petersen, S., et al. *Science News,* Vol. 138, No. 9, p. 134, Sept. 1, 1990.

11. Rachman, S., and Whittal, M. "Fast, Low and Sudden Reductions in Fear." *Behavior Res. & Ther.,* Vol. 27, No. 6, pp. 613–620, 1989.

12. Robins, L., Helzer, J., Hesselbrock, M., and Wish, E. "Vietnam Veterans Three Years After Vietnam: How Our Study Changed Our View of Heroin." *The Yearbook of Substance Use and Abuse,* Vol. 2, Eds. Brill, L., and Winick, C. Human Sciences Press, 1980.

13. Szasz, T. *The Untamed Tongue.* La Salle, Ill.: Open Court, 1990.

14. Wade, Joel. *The Effects of the Callahan Phobia Treatment Technique on Self-Concept.* Doctoral dissertation. Professional School of Psychological Studies, San Diego, 1990.

15. Walther, David. *Applied Kinesiology,* Vols. 1 and 2. Abriendo, Col.: Systems DC, 1981.

16. Walther, David, *Applied Kinesiology: Synopsis.* Abriendo, Col.: Systems, DC, 1988, p. 396.

About the Authors

D̲ᴿ. Rᴏɢᴇʀ Cᴀʟʟᴀʜᴀɴ, a clinical psychologist, maintains a practice in Indian Wells, California, but has treated patients all over the United States and Europe with his pioneering telephone treatment. He has appeared on "Donahue," "Oprah," "Good Morning America," and other television programs successfully demonstrating his techniques.

P̲ᴀᴜʟ Pᴇʀʀʏ, former Executive Editor of *American Health Magazine,* is the author of Healing Your Heart: A Proven Program for Reversing Heart Disease and co-author of the bestselling *Closer to the Light.*